YOUR ACHING BACK

AND WHAT YOU CAN
DO ABOUT IT

YOUR
ACHING BACK

AND WHAT YOU CAN
DO ABOUT IT

By David Shuman, D.O.

Past President, Philadelphia County Osteopathic Society; Head
of Department of Osteopathic Therapeutics, Juniata Park Medical Center; Secretary of Osteopathic College of Joint Sclerotherapy; Member of Board of Directors of Blue Cross

AND

George R. Staab

of the Philadelphia *Evening Bulletin* Staff

ILLUSTRATED BY JAMES H. BLUETT

GRAMERCY PUBLISHING COMPANY
NEW YORK

This edition is published by
Gramercy Publishing Company, a
division of Crown Publishers, Inc.

j   k   l   m   n   o   p   q

Manufactured in the United States of America.

CONTENTS

YOUR ACHING BACK

AND WHAT YOU CAN
DO ABOUT IT

PREFACE

Many friends have taken a kindly interest in this book. In most instances, their advice, suggestions and criticisms have been extremely useful, and as such gratefully accepted. Others have been firmly rejected as not consonant with the single objective to which the authors have addressed themselves: the better understanding by the general public of the human back and its problems, with particular regard to those readers to whom the subject may be both personal and painful.

One admittedly tempting suggestion the authors turned down seems to warrant at least some passing discussion. "Since Dr. Shuman is an osteopathic physician," some asked, "why not let the book elaborate on those aspects of the osteopathic-medical controversy involved?"

Aside from the fact that Dr. Shuman would not presume to speak for the entire osteopathic profession, there was another, and far more cogent, reason for the unwillingness of the authors to approach the material in this book from so limited a standpoint. For one thing, they reasoned, any hopeful reader seeking some help to escape the torment of a back disorder isn't at all likely to be much concerned with still another of those doctrinaire disputes among practitioners of the healing arts. Rather, he wants merely to get well and free from pain.

And rightly so.

Accordingly, the authors of this volume have sought to deal with the subject from that standpoint alone. As a result, the reader will find frequent references in these pages to conservative medical experience wherever and whenever necessary, strictly upon its merit. Happily, the medical profession has contributed a great deal of priceless research and sound thinking to the world's fund of knowledge in the healing arts, here as elsewhere. By the same token, no responsible physician of any sort would pretend for a moment that all is known.

As much as anything else, the authors have attempted to evaluate what is known, to reappraise existing practices and direct attention to some less-known improvements. Philosophical "party-lines" have been crossed indiscriminately, in favor of a practical, common-sense attitude and a search for the best, wherever found.

But lest there be the slightest misunderstanding, the present authors do not intend to mince words or spare error, regardless of how well entrenched or imbedded in accepted practice such error may be. Flatly, Dr. Shuman regards traction, adhesive strapping, diathermy, body casts, and disk operations as useless or worse. Just as flatly, this book is dedicated to the superiority over these of rest, manipulation, joint sclerotherapy, and curare, and the authors have set out to explain why.

In the words of Sir William Drummond: "He who will not reason is a bigot; he who cannot is a fool; and he who dares not is a slave."

THE AUTHORS

1. A FEW BACK FACTS

EVEN MONEY says there's a backache in your future. The odds go for just about anybody and everybody.

You don't have to be anybody special to get a backache. All you have to do is have a back, and who doesn't?

Backaches are no respecters of persons—the preacher and the chorus girl, the truck driver and the professor, the short-order cook, the housewife, the plumber, the necktie salesman, and the doctor, too, get a backache now and then. One is too many.

About the only group of people in the world who are exempt in any way from the common curse of an aching back are adherents to certain religious ideas for whom neither pain, backaches, nor anything else of a troublesome nature have any existence. These may wish to stop reading right now, assuming they've started. But for most of us, backaches are very real, too frequent, mighty uncomfortable, and no laughing matter, even if we try.

The whys and wherefores of backaches are almost as numerous as backs, but all kinds have one thing in common: nobody wants one.

Certainly the common backache has been with us at least as long as backs, which would run it back to the first appearance in the world of vertebrates. How and by what process our backs got to be the way they are is one for the anthropologists to wrangle about. This volume will concern itself solely with backs as we find them now, especially with backs in trouble, and with what can be done about them.

Despite the increasing incidence of backaches, there's no question but that the human back, given proper care and rightly understood, is an astonishingly effective mechanism. As much as the more frequently lauded human brain, the human back is the hallmark of our true nobility and a major factor in the long-developing supremacy of the animal, man.

Basically, the human back is a framework, either flexible or rigid as needed, from which every other organ— the legs, arms, head, and tail, if any—is suspended or otherwise supported and to which the entire body is related one way or another. Its principal member, the backbone, is just about the first piece of working machinery the embryo gets itself as it develops into somebody's child. Its magnificently organized system of nerves and neurological networks directly controls every function of the body from the neck on down, as well as a few more from the neck up. Its beautifully fitted bones, called vertebrae, are sturdily linked, each to each, by some of the strongest, toughest ligaments to be found anywhere in the body.

Because of them the human being, beyond all other creatures, may stand erect, his hands freed of the necessity of supporting him at rest or in motion. Aided by his freed hands and the cunning of his brain, man has come, as commanded in Genesis, to have dominion over all the earth.

Both hands and brain depend upon the back. Truly, your backbone is the backbone of human dignity.

And by the same token, your personal backbone, the one that gets the aches you're likely to have the most interest in, is as much as any other the one part of the body that can make you or break you. Oddly enough, to most people it is also one of the least familiar parts, even setting aside, for the moment, the fact that it is the one most people see the least of. Out of sight, out of mind.

But whether you see it or don't, one thing is sure. Your back is a truly marvelous hunk of machinery, an amazingly durable arrangement ready to serve the purposes of a ditch-digger or a banker, a prize fighter or a stenographer, equally well.

The same back that holds you conveniently erect while balancing a teacup at an afternoon party can quickly convert itself into a powerful derrick for shoveling snow, spading the garden, or pushing the furniture around.

But, unless you're looking for trouble, you'll give your back

a chance. Nobody would expect a banker to step from behind his desk and match a husky gravedigger at heaving dirt out of a six-foot hole without also conceding the banker a good chance of becoming a candidate for personal occupancy of the finished grave. And, you can't expect your back, upon which you have been relying to help you lift nothing heavier than a knife and fork, to take on instantly a furniture mover's job.

It may, if you're lucky. If you're not, you'll get yourself a first-class backache at least, and you may do permanent damage.

Along with the physical work it does, your back unmistakably reflects your frame of mind at any given moment.

When that "good one" you put your money on in the seventh at the racetrack comes in last, your back slumps in sympathy with your wallet. But when you barrel out of the boss's office with the word about how there'll be an extra

ten in the envelope next week, the old back snaps erect with pleasure.

"Stiffen your back," has become another way of saying "Get in there and fight," or "Buck up, Bub."

It's your back that gets the pats when you're out in front, and it's also your back that gets the boot when things are different. Nothing can better make a loser look like a winner than the mere business of straightening up the old back.

And there's a lot more to it than a matter of looks.

For hard-cash fact, back ailments add up to millions paid out each year by insurance companies in workmen's compensation payments, doctor bills, and general insurance claims of all kinds, including legitimate ones.

Questionable insurance claims—generally along the lines of how the poor fellow was on a trolley, for instance, and got jolted off his feet by a sudden stop, hurt his back, and can't work any more—constitute a big part of the medico-legal work in any insurance company.

There isn't a doctor alive who can be reasonably certain, despite X rays, reflex tests, palpation, and every clinical gimmick in the book, that a suspected fake doesn't have an injured back. So long as the poor fellow howls convincingly, his anguished yelps outrank the best scientific evidence anybody can get up. As often as not, and too often, the insurance company is stuck, and knows it.

But proving it is something else again, which sets the stage for the shake.

The exact dollar loss in missed pay envelopes directly traceable to ailing backs—whether they just got that way or followed an accident of some kind—is practically incalculable. A bum back can lay you up for a day, or for life. While you're stretched out in pain, your wife may have to step back into the job you married her away from. Your backache can cost your kids that college education you always figured on, and it can leave you a despondent, helpless cripple.

You can, perhaps, get by on your job with a gastric ulcer, let's say, or a kidney complaint, or even a dubious heart. But if your back fails, you're out of business entirely.

Entirely, in this connection, may mean sexually as well. Sexually, the situation for a man with "lumbago" is obvious. Not so obvious, however, is the very real possibility that a lot of the embarrassment, frustration, and missed opportunity caused by what doctors call impotence may well be due to a failing back. Infertility for the same reason is also not uncommon.

For a woman, the same obvious mechanical handicap needs no further explanation. Beyond this, any existing back condition, besides being painful, may well complicate the whole process of childbearing. It can seriously impair her ability to bear down during actual labor, and even more than in the male, a deficient back can contribute greatly to infertility.

Such being the case, it is astonishing, not to say dangerous, just how little most people, beginning with some doctors, know about backs—what they are, how they work, how we can get the most out of them, how to take care of them, and how to fix them.

As human machinery goes, your back is no more of a mystery than many other organs and structural components of your body. And, in many respects, your back is a lot less of a mystery.

There are, to be sure, some conditions—such as cancer of the spine, or osteitis condensans, an inexplicable, pernicious hardening of the bones, or Scheuermann's disease, a basically inflammatory proposition—about which nobody knows anything like enough to matter.

Fortunately these, and the like, present only a very minor portion, certainly less than 1 per cent, of the over-all problem.

Actually, there is presently more than enough sound, well-established scientific knowledge not only to alleviate but to cure almost any back ailment you can get.

As of now, physicians are well acquainted with the general physical attributes of your back. The muscles in it, each little bone and ligament, the nerve network directly associated with it, the glandular relationships involved, the mechanics of the entire area, as well as the detailed functions of each minor part, have been studied ever since the days of Aesculapius, named in Homer's *Iliad* as "the peerless leech."

Admittedly, up until about seventy-five years ago the medical profession was more deeply absorbed in staking out landmarks against such immediate threats as smallpox, syphilis, tuberculosis, yellow fever, and the like, and in scoring some very impressive wins against them.

But until comparatively modern times, doctors paid the human skeleton not much more mind than did Aesculapius.

With a lot more success than could be expected, doctors treated such easily determined complaints as broken bones and dislocated joints. Most of the information on the subject available to the old-timers came from studies of wired-up skeletons, still in use in medical school classrooms, and experience.

As far as the records show, nobody ever got such back diseases as osteoporosis, herniated nucleus pulposus, or "slipped disk," or hypermobile sacroiliac because, except for a handful of specialists, most doctors had never heard of them. Their patients got "lumbago."

The word lumbago means nothing more than a pain in the lumbar region, which amounts to telling a tubercular patient that he has a cough. The doctor might prescribe a mustard plaster or snuggling up in bed with a flannel-wrapped hot brick, or again he might respond with a sympathetic shake of the head and advise his patient to "take it easy for a while."

As often as not, the patient made out nearly as well by handing the operator of a traveling medicine show half a buck for a family-sized bottle of "Chief Lame Duck's Universal Pain Killer and Reliable Hair Oil."

Along about the mid-1800's, however, medicine in general had taken a definitely scientific cast. Increasingly, the outstanding professional minds of the time were turning to the laboratory, to controlled research and to a re-evaluation of the entire body of medical know-how then at their disposal. One of these, Dr. Andrew Taylor Still, finally came up with a revolutionary idea. Son of a Methodist Episcopal minister who was himself a frontier physician, Still was born in Jonesboro, Lee County, Virginia, August 6, 1828, the third of six children.

In 1852, young Dr. Still participated in the far western explorations of General Frémont as scout surgeon. At the close of the Civil War, in which he was wounded, Dr. Still relinquished his commission as a major in the Twenty-first Kansas Militia and resumed practice, applying the recognized principles of medicine then in common use. His break with the main body of medical practice came in 1874, and in 1892 Dr. Still founded his own school at Kirksville, Missouri. He died in 1917.

The human body, Still maintained, is fairly well equipped by its very nature to combat a good many, if not all, of the ailments likely to afflict it.

His thinking in this respect clearly foreshadowed the advent in modern medical practice of increasing reliance on antibiotics. In effect, an antibiotic is merely an induced boost given to bolster comparable substances produced naturally by your body. So reinforced, these natural substances can accomplish more effectively their appointed function in killing off harmful microbes, viruses, germs, and "bugs" of all kinds.

18

Endocrinological science has definitely established that, when he said that the body itself can produce its own remedies, Dr. Still was on the main track. Today the endocrinologist attacks a whole series of physical disorders through the endocrine glands. These glands are now known to be the source of one class of those benign substances Dr. Still was talking about.

What's more, Still insisted, unless the bony substructure of the entire body, meaning the bones of the skeleton and especially those of the spine, were in a natural and proper relationship with each other and everything else, good health could be regarded only as a highly unlikely accident.

Furthermore, he added, the medical profession, of which he was himself a member, could get along much better without nearly all of the doses, pills, concoctions, brews, potions, tonics, herbs, teas, essences, and powders then in use. In short, about 90 per cent of the stuff on the drugstore shelves, along with the Universal Pain Killer, were just so many medical mistakes salvaged from medieval magic. Dr. Still quit using them then and nobody uses them now.

Still promptly became very unpopular with both druggists and his fellow physicians, but not with his many happy, cured patients. The years since have shown, of course, that like those of many other pioneers, some of Dr. Still's ideas just didn't stand up, and they wound up in the same ash can with hundreds of other generally held mid-Victorian notions. But his analysis of the importance of the spine is still the basis of any hopeful approach to your aching back. And his insistence, that the sacroiliac is naturally a movable joint, contrary to the principles of anatomy then taught, is now accepted by all.

In the end, Dr. Still's disagreements with the general body of medical practice in his day led at last to the establishment of a new school of medical philosophy, which he called osteopathy. Some twelve thousand osteopathic physicians, surgeons, endocrinologists, neurologists, pediatricians, gynecologists, obstetricians, psychiatrists, and specialists of all kinds are now licensed in every state of the union. They staff hundreds of hospitals and serve as faculty in six colleges of osteopathy.

While Still was having it out with his professional opponents, a German scientist, Wilhelm Konrad von Roentgen, was getting ready to stumble across the X ray, one of the greatest diagnostic discoveries of all time. From 1895, the year Roentgen announced that passage of an electrically generated invisible ray through the body would trace bone pictures on a photographic plate, doctors were freed of a vast amount of guesswork. And Dr. Still's principles found a firm foundation.

More recently, the late Dr. Christian Georg Schmorl, the great Dresden pathologist, completed a series of studies on the spine and the intervertebral disks which are universally regarded as classics. Here in America, Dr. William Jason Mixter, and Dr. Joseph S. Barr, both of Massachusetts General Hospital, Dr. Henry William Meyerding and Dr. Ralph K. Ghormley at the Mayo Clinic, to name a few, have made vast contributions to what's known about your back.

It all adds up to better odds that you can avoid "lumbago" and, if not, escape most of its traditional miseries. The thoughts on the subject in this book are drawn from professional training and experience and, in a large measure, founded on what these men have learned.

2. BEHIND YOUR BACK—AND IN IT

TIME AFTER time patients ask why the doctor concerns himself with the spine when the pain may be in a leg or a shoulder, ankle, groin, foot, or maybe even in the belly.

In order for you to understand why, some basic knowledge of the anatomy and physiology of your back is a must. To begin with, except for twenty-four nerves called "cranial" because they run from your head, or cranium, all the nerves in your body run from your spine. Right now we're principally concerned with sixty-two big ones, which make up the central nervous system. Immediately on emerging from the spine, these nerves start dividing and redividing into finer and finer branches, reaching at last into every part of you, however tiny or remote. Nobody knows exactly how many separate nerves you've got in this system, but any one of them, right on down to the smallest, can raise royal Cain. Subject largely to the command of your brain, they call the turn for everything and anything you do.

Besides the nerves in the central nervous system, there's another group technically called sympathetic. This has nothing to do with feeling sorry for somebody with an aching back, which anybody ought to. Applied to this set of nerves, the word sympathetic might best be taken to mean automatic, because these nerves perform for you such jobs as blushing, sweating, heartbeat, digestion, and the like. They carry on without conscious mental direction on your part, but do depend a lot on what you're thinking. Anything that may go wrong with your spine, adversely affecting any of these main nerve lines in either the central or sympathetic group, will show up somewhere along the line. If the trouble hits a sympathetic nerve you may get asthma, let's say, or ulcers, constipation, palpitation of the heart. Or it may hit a nerve in the central system, and then you've got "lumbago." If you get it, you won't care much what anybody wants to call it so long as you can get rid of it.

Among these main nerve lines originating in the spine, two of them, called sciatic, account for by far the biggest problem involved in the more serious backaches. That word sciatic is one the Greeks gave us to describe the major nerve controlling each leg, and anybody with sciatica knows where it is from beginning to end.

The sciatic nerve starts just about under your hip pockets and runs right on down the middle of the leg, in the back, to the tip of your big toe. At the other end, near the spine, it is perhaps as thick as your finger and structurally as tough as an equally thick strip of rawhide.

It is formed by the convergence, or coming together, of five smaller nerves which emerge from the extreme lower portion of the spine—roughly, the part below your belt. These, plus a few more main nerves emerging from the spine a matter of inches above the belt line, are the ones most likely to get in the act when your back hurts. It's inflammation, or irritation, or damage of any kind to these nerves that makes itself known to you as a backache.

The spine itself, to which these nerves ultimately run, can also be the source of a full-scale pain in the back.

The spine is easily the most complicated and probably the

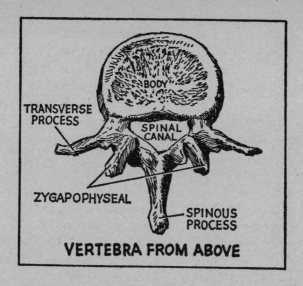

VERTEBRA FROM ABOVE

most misunderstood piece of bone and ligament assembly in all living bodies from fish on up. Yours is no exception.

Basically, the adult spine regularly comprises twenty-six oddly shaped, but generally flat, bits of bone sitting one on top of the other at the middle of your back. These bits of bone are called vertebrae.

Lying flat on a table, a typical vertebra would look generally egg-shaped, with three spurs or projections extending from the small end of the egg. If you'll reach back you can feel the middle spur from the outside, but those on either side of it are more deeply imbedded in muscle.

The one in the middle runs slightly downward, overlapping the vertebra below, so that all together these middle spurs protect your spinal cord in generally the same way that the overlapping shingles on the roof keep the rain out.

The side projections provide anchorage for the muscles used in bending or twisting your back.

Between the middle spur and those on either side, at the

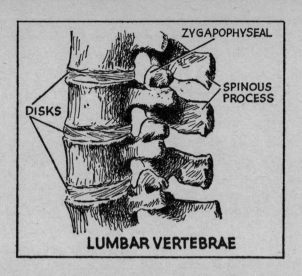

LUMBAR VERTEBRAE

root end each vertebra has four flat, very smooth bone surfaces, roughly about half an inch in diameter. These are called articular facets, and you'd better not lose track of them because they are important connections between the vertebra we're looking at and the ones above and below it. What's more, they're the villains in a large part of the backache plot.

Running right through the vertebra from top to bottom, close to and just in front of that middle spur, there's a hole. The hole of each vertebra, lined up with the corresponding holes in all the other vertebrae in your spine, make up a continuous tube or pipe, called the spinal canal. This canal contains, of course, the spinal cord.

The other part of the vertebra that needs to be remembered is the main area in what would be the big end of the egg. Doctors call this particular portion the body of the vertebra.

This body of the vertebra is the main weight-bearing portion, or platform, on which the vertebra above it rests, sharing the load with those articular facets we were talking about. It's a sort of tripod arrangement in which the facets act as secondary props, widening the over-all base. As the part with the heavy work to do, the body of the vertebra comprises a good half of its whole bulk.

When the vertebrae are assembled for business, each one is separated from the next by a cushion of ligament, tissue, and cartilage, surrounding the nucleus pulposus. (For the present, just think of nucleus pulposus as a blob of semi-liquid material about the size of a marble.) These cushions are called disks.

A pair of tough, cartilaginous plates, roughly circular, like the body on which the cushion rests, form the top and bottom of the cushion. Between these plates, the disk resembles a doughnut, the kind with a hole in the middle, and is made up of strong ligaments tying each vertebra to the next. That blob of stuff, nucleus pulposus, exactly fills the hole of the doughnut.

These disks and the vertebrae make up the spine, or back-bone. If it's damaged, injured, diseased, or otherwise out of whack, you're going to hurt, but good.

But the spine is not the whole works.

At its bottom end it rests on a tricky combination of three more bones, which pretty nearly everybody's heard about, talked about, and may even know something about.

One is called the sacrum and the other two are the ilia.

Teamed up, they provide the term sacroiliac, the three-piece combination of the sacrum, which is a roughly trian-gular middle part, plus one ilium on each side of it. Anybody who prefers English to Latin can just call these ilia the hip bones.

In roughly the same way in which auto shock absorbers keep the bumping of the wheels from pounding the body above, the sacroiliac cushions the shock produced by your

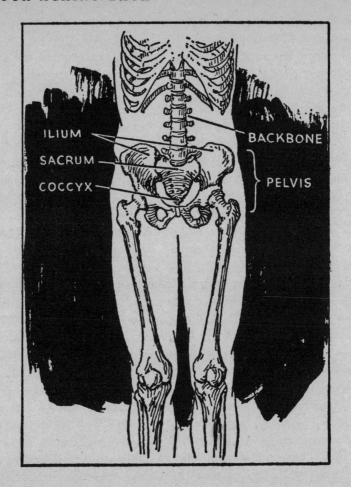

ILIUM

SACRUM

COCCYX

BACKBONE

PELVIS

pounding feet and so protects your upper body and its vital organs.

Your hip bones are almost without exception the most irregularly shaped, and also among the biggest bones you've got. Looking at one head-on, it has an outline very much like your ear only much bigger—no matter how big your ears may be. But, for the job it has to do, no engineer ever doped out a better design.

On one side, corresponding to the outer edge of the ear lobe, it makes a perfect ball-and-socket joint, allowing your legs to swing in pretty nearly any direction and permitting the development of such phenomena as rhumba dancers, marathon roller-skaters, six-day bike riders, and bird walkers.

On the inner side, the hip bone is attached to the sacrum. This sacrum is another structural dilly. Actually, it's made up of five small vertebrae, separate at birth. As the child grows up, these vertebrae grow together and fuse into one three-cornered piece, with the point down.

The biggest vertebra of your spine sits on the upper, rather flat side of this triangular sacrum, and so carries the weight of everything from there on up.

For all practical purposes, the spine and the sacroiliac joint are the main actors in the sad tale of an aching back. But, just for the record, there's another bit player that gets itself in the act once in a while—at least often enough to rate a second look. The fancy name for this one is the coccyx. Like the sacrum, it's made up of from three to five small vertebrae which fuse together. Not quite as long as your little finger, it hooks onto the lower point of the sacrum with a slightly movable joint. It provides an anchorage for some small muscles essential to the control of bowel movement.

There are enough profound thinkers around to lend some substance to the idea that the coccyx is what's left of the tail we may have had before we came down out of the trees, but no matter what, when you offer somebody a kick in the tail, that's the target. However, unless you're the target for somebody else, or, unless you try to sit down where there isn't any chair, it seldom gives much trouble of the kind we're talking about.

There, then, are the key items in the package—nerves,

vertebrae, disks, sacroiliac, and coccyx. The assembled vertebrae, with a disk cushion between each, comprise the spine.
Joined with the assembly on which it rests, the sacroiliac
combination, the two form the foundation of your back.

For the rest of it, there's a muscle system, including some
of the most powerful in your body. Numerous ligaments and
cartilages tie the main foundation of bones, spine, and sacroiliac together. Tendons, large and small, long and short,
attach the muscle system to this foundation or framework.

It all amounts to a mechanism that can bend and twist,
turn and squirm, shake and wiggle as we desire. And, just as
easily, it can stiffen up, hold itself put in any position and
exert top power when we need it.

Given proper care, a fair shake, and just a little understanding, your back will take on any job you ask of it, including the basic job of carrying you around on your feet.
When it fails, in practically all of the most severe cases the
failure is due to some sort of weakness in the various joints
between vertebrae of the spine, the spine and its sacrum, the
sacrum and the hip bones, singly or in any combination.

Such an unhappy condition is classified as instability, and
is a sure shot to kick up lumbago, sciatica, or the miseries,
eventually.

The rough idea is that instability is the chief reason why a
lot of us are having a pretty rough time of it.

3. FACING UP TO YOUR BACK

THE THORNY, pain-paved path facing you as you hurry to your favorite doctor—or, supposing you haven't any, then to the great guy your neighbor told you about—is one all too familiar to too many people. And the routine for getting over the visit is very much the same for all.

As a patient, you hobble into the doctor's office to wait your turn if you don't have an appointment, or get sore about having to wait anyhow if you have one and the doctor is delayed. After a while the inner door flies open, the doctor pokes his head into the waiting room and politely invites you in.

You lower your quivering frame carefully and gently into a chair beside his desk.

"Now, sir—" he begins. From there, like as not, he goes into a lot of trivia that ought to interest only the census-taker—things like your name, age, address, what you do for a living. Since you've come because of a back ailment, that question can be very, very important.

Don't get impatient. Sooner or later he'll get around to the payoff question—the one you've been waiting for.

"Now, sir," he'll ask at last, "what's bothering you?"

Now's your chance to tell him—and how! "Doctor," you

moan, "my back hurts. Awful. I can't walk. Just sitting here nearly kills me."

Then you'll reach back to show him the spot. "Right there, doctor."

If you're the talky type you may run on and on about what your wife said when you told her about it, and about some other guy you heard about who had a bum back, and anything else that occurs to you, but the chances are, as soon as you stop, the doc will want to know the answers to some specific questions. And it's going to help a lot if you still have wit enough, in spite of the way your back hurts, to come up with some of the answers. The nearer right, the better.

For instance, how did this attack start? When? What were you doing at the moment? Does bending over make it any worse? What happens when you cough? Or sneeze? Does lying down give you any relief? Is it there in the morning when you hop out of bed? Or, does it build up through the day? Or maybe it's going good as you struggle into your clothes in the morning and wears off as the day wears on?

If this isn't your first attack, when was the last one? How many have you had? And when, if you remember, did you get the first? Does the pain run down one leg? Both legs? Is it a sharp one like a knife cut, or a dull one like a thump with a baseball bat?

What, if anything, were you doing about your back before you got smart enough, or hurt enough, to come here? Mustard plasters? Liniment? Aspirin? Old Skullbuster rye? Obviously, since you're here, none of them worked.

While all this is going on, about the only notion in your head of any immediate importance to you is going to be the one you started with when you mumbled, "Doctor, my back hurts."

But there's a sound reason for most of the quiz routine you're getting now, all having to do for the most part with that stability business we mentioned before. Sooner or later, you're going to ask some questions of your own, such as, "How did I get that way to begin with?"

The ordinary customer sweating it out with a severe back-ache usually has only one prime idea: "Stop this hurting." You're not likely to be wasting much thinking on trying to figure out what's causing the misery. That's the doctor's job, anyhow. But when you are ready to wonder and ask, the chances are he'll answer with just one word: "Instability."

Like most other doctor-talk, that one needs explaining, though for once the word means just what it says. It means that something has become unstable, loose, weak, wobbly, floppy, and no longer capable of holding itself or anything else in place.

The "something" hit by the instability he's talking about will be the flock of joints in your spine, or the two much bigger joints in your dear old sacroiliac, or both.

For any one of a number of reasons—such as how you grew up, or an accident perhaps, or you may even have been born that way—one or more of these intricate and vital joints in your back has gone bad and stopped working the way it was intended to.

For instance, the joint setting up the commotion may be in your spine between two of those vertebrae you've already read about. Maybe one or more of these facets never grew to full size, and now that you're grown up, heavier, and by no means as spry as you used to be, the undeveloped facet can no longer carry its share of the entire load on the vertebra at the joint in question.

A heavy fall, a severe wrench, or a direct blow of any kind on the spine may stretch, or even rip loose, one or more of those all-important ligaments holding the entire spinal system in its proper relationship with the rest of you. The accident may or may not be covered by insurance, but all the money in the world won't prevent you from winding up with another example of what the doctor means by the word instability.

It could even happen, if you're good and unlucky, that you were born with a vertebra in which that hole, making up its part of the spinal canal, is in trouble. Some of us come up with a vertebra in which the hole, known technically as the vertebral foramen, has gaps on each side, or maybe only on one side, permitting the back half of the vertebra to separate, more or less, from the body or front part. It's not hard to see that such a vertebral joint would be weak and wobbly.

Now and then an individual turns up with an extra vertebra in the lower section of the spine, and, while the spare may give him more backbone, it doesn't actually work out that way. The condition generally results in an overflexible, whippy, flabby spine just where the greatest structural strength is needed. Instability again.

Such unfortunate situations, you may well guess, are only a relatively small but nonetheless important part of the picture. There are lots more. Nearly everybody has heard of another kind of difficulty that gets into the story—disks. Let's hope you only hear of it and never personally experience a bad disk.

The common disk failure is, in the end, merely another aspect of instability. Usually, what's happened has been the failure, from whatever cause, of the ligaments comprising that doughnut-like ring of the disk described earlier. These ligaments run between the plates in a sort of circular basket-weave pattern. Disk failure is so important that it is going to get some very special treatment in this book.

Admittedly, none of all this matters too much to you while you're sitting there on the chair answering questions. For you—and who can blame you?—the big deal is that backache.

It's hard to realize, but your agony isn't of more than passing interest to the doctor.

The better a doctor he is, the more likely he'll be to take a coldly professional view of your moans, sweating brow, trembling lips, and other evidences of acute grief you may display. In short, for the doctor, your pain is merely a symptom.

If he's enough of a scientific brute, he may even blandly explain that all pain, including yours, is a very fine thing indeed because it has drawn attention to something wrong, so that something can be done about it. Don't mind him on this score because he's right again. Besides, your friends, and perhaps even your spouse, will give you all the gratifying,

but pathologically useless, sympathy you'll want. What you want from your doctor is some information and advice on getting well, and that is, or should be, all he has on his mind for the moment.

He may even start probing into your sex life, for instance —whether or not you're still interested in romance, or have been noticing any functional irregularities. Or how often do you have to use the bathroom at night? Strictly private stuff like that.

The girls may think they're wearing the latest two-way stretch because it keeps their curves in the right places. But doc isn't thinking of that when he may ask his patient, "Do you feel better with your girdle on or off?"

Are you constipated? How about your digestion? Appetite? When you throw a tantrum or blow your stack, do you end up with the old backache? How do you get along with the weather? Pain when it's sloppy? Maybe feel better on fine days?

When he finally seems to have run out of questions, he'll at last get around to looking at that back you've been trying to draw his attention to. A man patient will be asked to strip from the waist up; women patients climb into a light examination gown, split up the back.

With the patient standing up, the doctor gazes over the battlefield where all the little devils are banging away. He'll want you to bend thus and so, while he gropes around with his hands, feeling muscles and motions.

Then on the table. Out comes the little rubber hammer, and your reflexes get a going over. When you're flat on your back, he may ask you to raise first one leg and then the other straight up. The way your back is acting up, you may think this will kill you, but it won't.

When he's had enough of this byplay, the doctor will lapse into a contemplative period. He may remember to tell you,

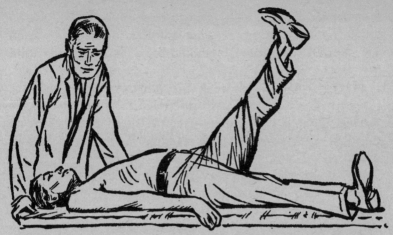

without being asked, that you may now put your clothes on.

Along with all the rest of the possibilities previously mentioned, his highly trained mind will be hopping around things like spasm, bone disease, referred causes, instability, and structural faults. Out of the lot he'll decide which of the many possibilities fit you, and that is your diagnosis. Both of you can start hoping he's right.

When his reverie is over, since he is at heart a very nice guy, he may recall something you were saying about how you hurt and get around to something for your immediate relief. It may take the form of a hypodermic injection of an exotic drug called curare, or one of the general painkillers like Demerol, Dromoran, procaine, or even morphine.

On the other hand, another doctor you pick may strap your back with broad bands of adhesive tape, which will be no fun at all getting off later, or he may try some diathermy, which means he'll hook you up to a mysterious electric cabinet that looks something like a radio console with a pair of mechanical-monster arms. It sends a deeply penetrating heat ray into the affected area, which may fool you into thinking you don't hurt any more.

35

It could even happen that you get a prescription calling for a souped-up variety of a well-known remedy, much advertised on TV, called aspirin and, for good measure, he tells you to go back home and get into the bed you climbed out of to come see him.

If you admit being strong enough in the wallet to afford the best, your doctor may want further tests of one kind or another and send you around to a clinical laboratory for them. He's almost certain to want some X-ray shots.

If your doctor is an osteopath, there's still another procedure available, provided your trouble turns out to be the kind where osteopathic manipulation, or a treatment, can help. If you're lucky enough to fall into this category, you may be pleasantly surprised at the results, which is another way of saying maybe you'll stop hurting right away.

At this point you've spent anywhere from five bucks on up—and the up can run as high as twenty-five dollars for the doctor's fee—something like forty-five minutes to an hour of your time, and you and your doctor ought to have a pretty good idea of just what goes. Every once in a while a backache patient can get by on just one visit to his doctor. With that kind of luck it's hard to imagine how he ever got his "lumbago" to begin with. Almost as rarely, a week or so in bed, a heating pad perhaps, and the tender ministrations of the folks at home may turn the trick. But by far the majority of low-back patients are in for a longer pull.

The unluckiest may face one of the most delicate and doubtful pieces of surgery in the book—a disk operation. Even the toughest, strictly professional, this-is-my-duty doctor in the world isn't anxious to recommend this one. It's unpleasant to read about, unpleasant to hear about, and ten million more times unpleasant to endure.

But the disk problem can't be dodged, and this book doesn't intend to. Let's look this disk right in the eye.

4. THE DISK AND ITS PROBLEMS

OF ALL THE backaches around that can be blamed on instability, the one you get from a bad disk is among the worst. What's more, faulty disks are by far the biggest source of back trouble considered from a percentage standpoint. Along with those cases definitely identified during diagnosis as disk problems, there is another uncounted number which are really disk problems, although not yet far enough developed to show up as such.

As often as not, a man will get along fairly well for a time with such a slight disk disorder, provided it's slight enough. A good deal depends on the nature of his work. For instance, a chair-bound clerk, bank president, or Pentagon general can get by with a weakened disk that would put a carpenter, a gravedigger, or a stevedore out of business fast.

But, no matter what, unless it's tended to, the slightly damaged disk will certainly become a badly damaged one, beyond ignoring, in due course of time.

Disk trouble can be found in patients of almost any age up to seventy or more, but most of it turns up in men in their forties. No case has ever been reported of a child under ten having a bad disk, and there have been relatively few teen-agers so afflicted. In three cases out of four, Pop has the trouble rather than Mom, which shows something about who's doing the heavy slugging for the family. A good deal of the disk trouble is the result of direct accident, and the rest generally follows strains encountered in heavy lifting, shoving, heaving, hauling, and similar strong-arm stunts.

As far back as the days when De Soto, Cortez and Pizarro were exploring the wonders of newly discovered America, a man named Vesalius was something of a medico-surgical wonder back in Padua. He had a pretty good idea of what a disk amounted to, but he had had to resort to some shady deals to find out.

In those days people took a dim view of the business of carving up cadavers to find out what was inside, and most of the anatomical investigation going on before Vesalius' time was done on the carcasses of dead animals. Dissection of dead people was regarded with horror, though the application of the rack, thumbscrews, and branding irons on live ones was a common spectacle on public holidays as free entertainment for all. Vesalius upset a lot of people by his insistence upon taking human corpses apart to see what had made them tick. When he had trouble getting a specimen, he wasn't above snatching the body of a hanged criminal right off the gallows.

But in the end Vesalius knew more about the inner workings of the human body than any man alive, and when he wrote his revolutionary book on the subject, called *Structure of the Human Body*, the disks were described with fair accuracy for the first time. Still, nobody then, starting with the doctors, had any notion of the part played by these disks in your aching back, and there's lots of arguing about this going on even today.

But there are a number of considerations about which there is no argument. For one thing, the failing disk is in trouble because those basket-weave ligaments making up the doughnut have been wrenched, torn, or otherwise damaged.

38

For another, that blob called nucleus pulposus, filling the center hole, has been squeezed out through the rupture, or weakened part of the disk. This is called a herniated disk.

Under these conditions your back hurts, either because the extruded nucleus in turn presses against a nerve emerging from the spine at the point in question, or, and more likely, the joint, unstable because of the ruptured ligaments of the ring, is irritated, congested, inflamed, and disturbed.

So it hurts in exactly the same way a dislocated or so-called trick knee hurts. It hurts for the same reason a sprained ankle, or wrenched shoulder, or twisted wrist hurts, without further reference to pressure on a nerve or any other consideration.

The pain so set up may confine itself to the injured area alone. Or, should any of those major nerves we mentioned—the sciatic, for example—get involved in the same irritation, congestion, inflammation, or disturbance, the nerve will also hurt and its pain will register in your legs. Under certain conditions you might not even report a specific pain in the back and mention only the far greater sciatic pain in the legs, but the back is still adversely affected by the instability set up in the damaged disk.

Back in 1896, a certain fellow took a hundred-foot nose dive, but straightened up in time to land on his feet. He was pretty tough and, reportedly, even managed to walk a few steps before falling down. But the jolt had shaken loose a lot of his abdominal machinery, such as the kidneys and intestines. This, the doctors figured, finally killed the poor fellow.

When somebody took a second, closer, and post-mortem look, a ruptured disk was also found—the first authenticated disk hernia in medical history. There has been a long line of them since, and the accident opened the way for detailed study of the ruptured disk as such.

By latest count, out of a given one thousand operations in Pennsylvania of all kinds, including circumcisions, some twenty-two were necessitated by disk trouble of one kind or another during 1952, according to the Medical Service Association of Pennsylvania. On a national scale, the Veterans Administration reports that out of 10,172 backache cases handled during 1952, no less than 5,082 (or nearly half of the total) were traced to faulty or degenerated disks.

Setting aside for the moment the damaged disks arising from direct accident, the condition ordinarily appears first as a mild, aching discomfort in the small of the back. At this point, most victims settle for a heating pad, some liniment, or an easy chair.

There may even be a realization that that little job of snow-shoveling or garden-spading just finished may have had something to do with it, but what's actually happened has been the beginning of the end. A few small fibers of ligament have been stretched or pulled beyond their capacity. Just the tiniest bit, of course, and, given a few hours rest, the ache is likely to go away. But the damage remains.

A few days, or maybe a week later, let's say, you're putting out the trash or ashes. This time the bang comes a little quicker, and stronger, because those fibers, not yet fully recovered from the garden-spading, are even weaker than they were the first time.

Things can go along like this for years, getting progressively worse, and lasting a little longer each time until the day you get a major collapse of the disk. This time neither liniment nor the heating pad nor climbing into the sack does any good. The pain going on is giant-size, and only the toughest victim goes to the doctor's office with it, for the very good reason that only a real tough guy can bear to move at all.

Most send for the doctor, and at this juncture about the

only thing the doctor can do is administer a hypodermic painkiller and offer a little discussion about disks. By this time the disk, starting with those few weakened fibers that caused the first little touch of lumbago, has broken down in a serious way. The central nucleus may be squeezed out through the rupture in the disk, and everybody involved is in for a very hard time indeed.

Beginning with you!

It's your deteriorated disk, and your agony. To be sure, your folks are also in for a hard time because you're going to be hard to live with. You are also due to lose a lot of time off the job.

As the star of this sad drama, you, the patient, will find yourself in bed, usually lying on one side, with the leg that hurts pulled up toward your chest. The tired, weary muscles of your back, straining to hold you in some position of comfort, will ache of their own account from the effort. A cough, or worse yet, a sneeze, will send fresh stabs of misery across the back and down the leg, so it's a good idea not to have a cold at the time.

If the damage to the disk is the result of an accident of some kind, a blow or a fall, there is what might possibly be considered as at least one small advantage—you get the works right away, without waiting, and so you can get started on the long job of getting well just that much sooner. As grim as all this sounds, all is not lost, including the fact that you are still alive, although maybe wishing you weren't.

Right off the bat you ought to know that some of the finest doctors in the land, such as the Mayo Clinic men, and medical scientists as far away as Sweden, too, have known cases every bit as serious as yours in which the doctor never did anything except make a diagnosis, and the patient got well.

Long periods of bed rest, as much as two months perhaps, followed by another long period of convalescence in which all weight was kept off the injured disk, did the trick. Nature got a chance to go to work, to absorb the extruded nucleus, to erect a new wall of fibrous ligament around the break and even, in some instances, to fuse together the adjacent vertebrae involved with a new bony growth. With the wobbly, unstable condition caused by the ruptured disk so rectified, the pain stopped.

Consider, for instance, one smart patient in the wholesale edible-nut business. Admittedly, he wasn't using his head much the day he stepped from his office to help out one of his hired hands with the nuts. He should have known lifting wasn't his line, but he started to hoist up a sack of filberts anyhow. That did it. He wound up in bed with a typical

herniated disk and all that goes with it. Faced with the alternatives, he elected the do-nothing method, operating his business over the phone from home. In something under eleven weeks he was back in the office—a little stiff perhaps, and willing to let the hired nut-lifters earn their pay without his help, but otherwise was well and free of pain, and he hasn't gone near a doctor since.

Such happy endings are admittedly rare, though the chances are they might occur more often if the sufferers were just a little more patient. For the most part, however, the situation demands action, which ordinarily means surgery. But before they would wheel you into the operating room, they would most likely go through some diagnostic investigative preliminaries equally delicate, hazardous, and painful.

Two such procedúres are in use: the myelogram and the nucleogram. They are performed to determine to what extent and in what direction the nucleus of the damaged disk has been forced or squeezed out through the wall of the dough-nut. To make the myelogram, a special dye is injected into the spinal canal near its lower end. An X-ray picture will then disclose at least any backward bulge caused by extrusion into the canal of the nucleus center.

In the second procedure, the nucleogram, a dye is hypo-dermically injected directly into the nucleus. An X-ray pic-ture will then reveal any distortion that may have taken place anywhere in the entire nucleus, thereby indicating just where within the disk the wall may have broken down.

As diagnostic measures, the myelogram and the nucleogram are in effect courts of the last resort. Successfully carried out, they will establish the facts clearly and accurately.

However, for the ordinary case there are numerous other adequate, less drastic diagnostic methods that serve quite well. What's more, they cost less, hurt less, and offer much less risk. The outward, easily identifiable, and hard-to-mistake signs of a ruptured disk seldom need confirmation by either myelogram or nucleogram before beginning treatment.

Once it's agreed that a disk—retropulsed, deteriorated, de-generated, herniated, ruptured—all of which mean plain busted—is the cause of it all, it then becomes important to find out just why you hurt the way you do. The actual hurt-ing comes about in one of two ways, or perhaps in both at once.

That soft inner core of the disk, the nucleus, has been squeezed out through the torn disk wall, something like tooth-paste out of a tube, and may be pressing directly on a nearby nerve emerging from the spinal column at the point in ques-tion. Or, and this is by far the more frequent problem, the general distortion and strain caused by the resultant instability, the shifting of unaccustomed loads to portions of the vertebral joint never designed to bear them—these, together or singly, set up the pain.

The basic situation, good for a lot of grief all by itself, gets a big help in the devilish work of making you miserable out of the very efforts your body makes to shield you. Once the pain begins, every ligament and muscle anywhere near the damaged disk is in trouble as well.

Nearby ligaments, suddenly called upon to take up the load abruptly dropped by the ruptured disk, are strained beyond their natural capacity in an unconscious effort to ease the pressure on the afflicted disk. So *they* hurt.

Some muscles too, such as the little ones not more than an inch long, which run from one vertebra to the next, get involved. The ruptured disk tends to flatten out, allowing the vertebrae to move closer together. Right away those little muscles tighten up, pulling mightily to prevent the vertebrae from shifting.

The psoas, one of the biggest muscles in your whole back, stretches from the small of your back right on down to your thigh. It, too, gets in the battle, trying along with the others to keep the affected vertebral joint from sagging, slipping, or twisting out of line. As a result, it also gets to hurting.

So strained, the muscles are said to be in spasm—a sudden, violent, and involuntary contraction in which the body tries to improvise a temporary support, or splint, for the failing disk. As often as not, the effort twists the entire upper torso out of shape, and the victim bends awkwardly to one side or another. It becomes impossible to sit or stand erect.

Actually, this "lumbago" is a tough rap, and admittedly no place for any Pollyanna stuff. But there are a number of treatments available, any one of which may come in a winner. In the main, you've got three choices.

You can use the do-nothing technique—keep the weight off and pray for some high-grade natural healing.

Or, you can go for some surgery, an operation called a laminectomy, plus perhaps another called arthrodesis, and pray for the kind of luck that will keep you out of that tragic percentage of cases which terminate by leaving the victim, to all intents and purposes, a hopeless cripple.

But best of all, short of not having any trouble of this kind to begin with, you may get a comparatively new type of treatment called sclerotherapy.

Of which, more later.

5. LOW-DOWN MOANIN'

WE NOW COME to the "Sacroiliac Blues," and anybody who wants to listen can hear 'em moanin' low, and loud too, in doctors' offices all the way from Outer Mongolia to Main Street, and from Istanbul to Patagonia.

Despite the world-girdling lament of unnumbered sacroiliac sufferers, there are still an astonishing number of medical men around, all of them legitimate holders of duly attested and properly framed licenses to practice, who blandly maintain even now that there just isn't any such thing as sacroiliac trouble.

This being the case, these practitioners can't possibly be interested in what happens when your vital sacroiliac joints jam up or otherwise fail. Stay away from such.

The fact remains that in a single year the Veterans Administration alone reported treating 1,326 cases under the heading "affection of the sacroiliac joint," all of them representing various long-standing ailments. They treated another 1,876 for immediate sprains and strains—sacroiliac ailments newly developed.

Anybody who has ever had a go-round with a sacroiliac acting up, knows that this type of backache is a horse-sized helping of double-dipped, pluperfect torment, whether or not the doctor in charge knows the score.

Fortunately, nobody yet has gone so far as to deny that you do have some joints of various kinds in your pelvic girdle, even if some won't admit that these joints can give trouble. You not only have a sacroiliac joint, but as a matter of demonstrable fact, you've got two of them.

It has somehow become common practice to regard the sacroiliac as a singular proposition only. People accordingly, and a lot of doctors too, generally speak of "the sacroiliac joint." It's just another small example of the kind of loose talk, a good deal of it coming from men who ought to know better, cluttering up the whole sacroiliac picture.

For instance, there's a whole string of pains, aches, agonies, and hurting in general originating below the belt. Most of it gets uncritically lumped under the term "sacroiliac trouble" when it isn't just as loosely charged off to our old fakir friend, lumbago.

The word sacroiliac has become a sort of low-back diagnostic catchall, covering just about anything and everything out of whack in the lower back area, including kidney disorders, prostate problems, and bed-wetting.

Inability to distinguish a genuine sacroiliac failure among the many closely related symptoms of other ailments has been a prolific source of much futile and feverish medical fandancing and surgical shadow-boxing.

The functions, make-up, and operational aspects of the sacroiliacs, not to mention the rest of the pelvis, have led to some cosmic brouhahas within the medical profession, most of which went over the heads of the laity, which, in the opinion of most of the battlers, couldn't be expected to understand what it was all about anyhow. So not too much leaked out on the subject.

By now, pretty nearly everybody's heard about Galileo and

his metaphysical-astronomical set-to with the authorities. Galileo, the story goes, got himself into all sorts of trouble with his inconvenient, bull-headed notion that the world moves around the sun. The idea, it seems, was extremely distasteful to the Official Thinkers of the period. The world, said they, didn't move at all, and Galileo ought to stop circulating such subversive nonsense. Long, long years after time proved Galileo right, a fairly comparable dispute broke out among members of the medical profession. The quarrel wasn't quite as dramatic, nor as well publicized, but it was certainly of equal, and possibly greater, immediate significance to the laity.

At the time, the accepted idea, firmly entrenched in the best conservative medical dogma of the day, was that the joints of the pelvis were rigidly fixed and immobile, including, of course, the sacroiliac.

When Dr. Still, then a relatively young and obscure physician, put his professional reputation on the line with a novel, unorthodox, but soundly conceived concept to the contrary, the commotion began.

As could be expected, there were contemporary anatomists, physiologists and high-priced professors of medicine by the hundreds, whose pelves fairly rattled at the mere notion of motion in the pelvis. Undismayed by their dismay, Still persisted in his anatomical intransigence. The joints of the pelvis, he firmly declared, were truly joints and, as such, moved.

Galileo had the right pitch about the world, and Dr. Still had the right pitch about the pelvis. But he made little progress in his efforts to clear things up for his contemporaries, and as a matter of record it wasn't until as late as 1919 that another physician, Dr. Edward W. Chamberlain, settled the argument.

Combining a few basic principles of physics with some fairly simple X-ray techniques, Dr. Chamberlain devised a method to demonstrate visibly the principles Dr. Still could only assert from logic, open-minded observation, and painstaking anatomical exploration. The failure by the medical fraternity of Still's day to accept the sacroiliac as a genuine, movable joint was a major mistake, and the lost ground it cost medicine has still to be made up.

Among other results has been the fact that, until relatively recent times, there has been far too little appreciation of the mechanics, functions, and general character of the pelvis. The sacrum, in particular, has seldom been accorded either the respect or the professional understanding to which it is definitely entitled as a critically important factor in the over-all low-back situation.

But the man or woman cursed with an honest, for-real sacroiliac problem hasn't a doubt in the world that this pain is without exception the lousiest of the whole lousy list.

One thing is now abundantly clear. The joints of the pelvis do have a normal, if limited range of motion, and when this motion is in any way circumscribed or impeded, a typically painful sacroiliac condition follows. As often as not, there's a violent accident, or damaging strain from an excessive, awkwardly managed lift in the background.

The overstrained sacroiliac joints may shift, however little, on one side or the other, or both. Soon after that, you and your doctor will be having a chat about sacroiliac slip. While he's putting you through the routine quiz program, you may even remember having heard a very definite click when the blamed thing went out—sounded something like what you'd hear if you snapped your fingers with gloves on.

It maybe started hurting like the dickens right away, or maybe it waited a day or so. By way of treatment, strapping of one kind or another, diathermy, or special belts may be prescribed, none of which will do the condition any particular harm.

Proper adjustment by a skilled osteopathic physician or a medical doctor can realign the bones, re-establish their normal relationships, and relieve the pain at once. Provided of course you really do have a genuine sacroiliac slip, and not something else your doctor may have mistaken for one.

Any doctor skilled enough to adjust a slipped sacroiliac properly is probably smart enough to identify one in the first place. Your story about how it hurts steadily, in bed and out, standing or sitting, is one important clue. If the seat of the pain is pretty close to the seat of your pants, plus a marked tenderness of the general area between the hip pockets, that's another.

With proper management, a simple sacroiliac slip is a relatively minor mishap, easily fixed and no problem. The trouble is, the straight, uncomplicated sacroiliac slip accounts for comparatively few of the low-back cases limping into the average doctor's office.

From a treatment standpoint, the procedure in a true slip is a specific one, certain to produce results, and no more of a chore than the setting of a broken bone. In almost every instance, such a slip has been at the bottom of the classic story about how an old fellow pushing eighty crawled into the doctor's office on crutches and bounced out again in no time at all to chase the girls around some more.

That's the way it can work out, *if*—and the if depends on a lot of good sense, good luck, good judgment, and good treatment. Otherwise, the outcome can be tragic.

Suppose you're the kind of optimist who just doesn't realize that here is something serious. You try to shrug it off on the theory that, since the pain came by itself, it will obligingly depart the same way. But of course it doesn't go away. So then you climb into bed with the heating pad and maybe take some good old aspirin.

But the pain hangs on. So the next day, or the day after that, when you've been hurting enough to get a little smarter, you see a doctor, who maybe turns out to be one of those guys who doesn't believe in sacroiliac slip. So you get treated for good old lumbago.

While the useless lumbago treatment is going on, the real trouble, undetected and neglected, can worsen to the point where the sciatic nerves become involved, sending belts of incredibly agonizing pain down either leg, or both legs at once. By this time, about the only out remaining is morphine or some other painkiller, and that's that until a completely new approach is made.

Let's hope your sacroiliac slip gets handled right the first time, when treatment is easy on everybody including the doctor.

Unhappily, however, by far the most sacroiliac trouble is of an entirely different and more difficult nature, falling under the broad classification of hypermobility. Hypermobility means too much motion and describes the appearance of instability in these highly important joints lying just above your backside.

When you get right down to it, that sacroiliac setup of yours is an astonishingly well-organized piece of business. The sacrum, roughly wedge-shaped, fits neatly in the space between your hip bones, for all the world like a keystone into a masonry arch.

All the weight in your upper body—the heavy head, your abdominal organs, and your arms, plus whatever loads you may pick up with them—is transmitted through the sacrum to your hips, through which the total load passes on to the powerful, heavy thigh bones below.

Your sacroiliac joints, located at the very point where the first load transference takes place, have a double function. For one thing, the cartilage lining these joints works in much the same way the disks work between vertebrae, giving you a cushion against the shock of your footsteps.

For another, these sacroiliac joints allow for the easy and unhampered swing of your legs from the hips. These joints are at the root of much of the romance in the world, because they have a good deal to do with the way a woman's hips move the way they do.

But of vastly greater significance, these ligaments of the sacroiliac offer a truly remarkable example of the profound harmony that threads its way through all nature. As the time nears for the pregnant woman to have her baby, these ligaments are ordained to loosen and relax, thus permitting the pelvis to accommodate to the climax of labor with the greatest freedom possible.

These ligaments should return to their former condition afterward, if all goes well, restoring to the sacroiliac joints the great strength they need for their job. But sometimes, usually in a woman who has had difficulty in childbearing, this fails to happen and the mother is left with a hypermobile sacroiliac.

Contrary to the kind of hurting produced by a sacroiliac slip, a hypermobile sacroiliac is often considerably relieved by nothing more than bed rest. Most women victims, and nobody knows how many men, feel better when wearing corsets. To some small extent, support by strapping will help —but not with adhesive tape.

By and large, such hypermobile joints, loose and wobbly because of weakened ligaments, tend to slip out of place far more easily than healthy, well-developed sacroiliacs. When such a slip occurs it can, of course, be easily adjusted, but permanent improvement in the general hypermobile condition requires other measures.

Currently, the commonest form of treatment utilizes a therapeutic belt, buckled or laced around the middle just below the belt line. It's comfortably warm in winter, and a sweaty nuisance in summer. One smallish Philadelphia belt shop alone turns out more than two hundred each week at anywhere from five dollars on up.

Actually, there's many an unsightly, middle-aged potbelly slung up under a sacroiliac belt, for which there isn't much other use.

For anybody who'll hold still, there's some surgery available. The usual caper is to graft a sliver of bone about six inches long, sawed out of your shin, onto the sacroiliac. A groove big enough to take this bone-graft is cut right across the joint from one hip bone to the other, and the hunk of shin slipped into place.

When they get you out of the cast after such an operation, you may be better or you may not. Certainly, you won't have any sacroiliac joints to speak of, though you may still have some annoying sacroiliac pain.

Besides an operation, there are a few other prospects, most of them just as dismal. You may find yourself treading a weary, dreary path leading from one doctor's office to another and spending long, pain-bathed hours roasting in diathermy machines. You can get rid of scads of dough on trick belts, internal prescriptions, and hypodermic shots of anything they can put in the syringe from the latest wonder drug to salicylates—otherwise aspirin—and get nowhere.

When you're through you'll have a family-sized album full of X-ray pictures, a close acquaintance with just about all the doctors and most of the druggists in town, and an endless fund of corny jokes you've been hearing from your friends. The good chances are that you'll still have your sacroiliac condition also.

6. SPONDY, SCOLY AND ZYGAPOP

THIS IS AS good a time as any to introduce spondylolisthesis.

One of the more devilish exhibits in the low back chamber of horrors, spondylolisthesis is every bit as nefarious and shifty as could be expected of something with a name like that. It's another of those word-steals from Latin and Greek so dear to the obscurantist medical mind. Translated, it simply means a slipping in the spine.

For the purposes of this book, from now on spon-dy-lo-lis-the'-sis will appear as merely spondy, which may not be very dignified but will certainly be more practical.

As an adequately disreputable member of the Backache Hooligans, spondy shares a very special distinction with one or two other members in good standing. If you've got spondy you were born with it.

It takes a bump or a thump, a heavy lift or an awkward twist to give you a bad disk or a load of sacroiliac grief. But spondy is acquired merely as a matter of bad luck at birth. Usually, by the time spondy begins to make its presence felt, there's not much chance of eliminating the cause. It's too late for that, though to a great extent, modern medicine has learned to alleviate even this hopeless affliction.

Slowly, persistently, and insidiously, the condition arising at birth develops according to a well-established pattern. It is seldom detected early enough to get preventive attention, even should such a procedure be possible. Early X-ray studies of children anywhere from two years old up could reveal the beginnings of spondylolisthesis, but such precaution is rare and of dubious value.

The disease develops inexorably.

Like most other disabilities of the back, the problem with spondy is primarily mechanical. It most often affects the lowest, and therefore largest, vertebra of the spine, technically known as the fifth lumbar vertebra. This is the one directly above the sacrum, serving as a sort of foundation stone for the rest of the vertebrae. Right from the beginning, the victim has a fifth lumbar vertebra in which the front, or body portion, is separated from the back part by gaps in the walls of the ring.

Occasionally, the fourth lumbar vertebra, which is the one next above, may be similarly afflicted.

At first it doesn't matter very much. The infant tumbles around in his bassinet without any outward indication of distress. As the years go by the bone structure of the growing child hardens up, but those gaps in the ring never join together, and the forward portion of this all-important foundation vertebra remains detached from the back portion.

Sometimes the trouble may not show up until the late teens. It appears with increasing frequency in the adult years, as the burdens of living, both literally and figuratively, come to bear. No one with spondy can hope to sneak through the years of maturity and old age without distress unless he's very, very lucky. Sooner or later, as the years go by, this maverick front portion of that all-important fifth vertebra begins to creep forward, slipping across the platform provided for it by the sacrum below. A hairsbreadth each week, or each month perhaps, steadily, relentlessly, the slipping goes on day and night. The deficient vertebra edges forward closer and closer to the brink of the pelvis. It no longer bears fully and firmly on the sacrum.

As it slides toward disaster, it carries the whole spinal assembly above it along the path of ever increasing distortion and displacement. Ligaments of the intervening disk, designed to serve other needs, are stretched and weakened by the shifting vertebra. Nearby nerve lines, caught in the increasingly abnormal conditions created over the years, become inflamed and irritated.

This is spondylolisthesis.

For what it's worth, spondy seems to have been among the curses afflicting mankind for a long, long time. The American Indian turns out to have been one of the early victims of spondy. No matter what the situation may be concerning our historical crimes against the American Indians, the incidence of spondy among them is one that can't be laid at the white man's doorstep.

As much as a quarter of a century ago, Dr. Russell Congdon, a fellow of the American College of Surgeons, ran an anatomical post-mortem check on about two hundred long-gone red men turned up by an archeological expedition working the Columbia River basin. Ten of the Indians, or five per cent of the sample, had spondy.

For these native-born savages, as well as the savages of a different order who replaced them, spondy is the same.

There is hurting, of course. This hurting, for all practical purposes, is exactly like the hurting that goes on when a disk is in trouble. Frequently, the pain is not present upon arising in the morning, but as the day wears on the pain builds up and the patient wears down. The sure evidence on spondy comes out in X-ray pictures.

As a matter of hard and unpalatable fact, no one insists that surgery can give much help. There just isn't any way to pull the wandering forward portion of the affected vertebra back into its proper position, even if there were any way to keep it there if it could be hauled back.

With a very delicate, dubious, and expensive bone-grafting operation, it is sometimes possible to connect two or three of the lowest vertebrae to the sacrum in the back, converting the entire lower area into a rigid, immobile assembly. This is done to prevent further shifting of the spine, and to enable it to support weight better. The unattached forward portion of the affected vertebra is ignored.

Or the surgeon may try a few tricks familiar to any carpenter, such as sinking a few metal screws into the vertebra which pin the back portions to each other above and below the trouble. This, everybody hopes, will provide somewhat better support for the torso. In this operation, as in the bone-grafting stunt, the free-floating forward part of the vertebra, which caused the trouble to begin with, is allowed to get lost.

The search for a sure-shot surgical method for dealing with spondy led to two fantastically spectacular operating-room experiments, still on the medical books as a prize example of what not to do when it comes to spondy. By special permission of the Royal College of Surgeons, these operations were performed on a pair of hard-luck patients who volunteered. Driven beyond endurance, they willingly consented to a desperate try at working up some surgical approach to the problem.

The strategy attempted in these cases was to come at the damaged vertebra through the abdomen. After slashing through the abdominal wall, the surgeons went on down through the intestines to lay open a gap exposing the spine at the sacrum. The loose frontal vertebra body was pushed back in place and a bone graft spliced in to hold it there.

One loyal British subject died right away, while the other unsung hero hung around a while in indescribable agony before he too, in God's mercy, died.

The operations made history. They have also been forever banned in England.

Outside of surgery, there remain only a very few other standard remedies for spondy, procedures usually offered for what they may be worth as an alternative to doing nothing at all. These consist primarily of belts, braces, and corsets of one kind or another, all recommended in the hope that this unstable, slipping vertebral joint between the spine and the sacrum can be supported from the outside somehow.

Candidly, there just isn't any cure for spondy.

At the very best it may be possible, by using advanced methods, to halt the disastrous creeping of that big bottom vertebra off its proper seat on the sacrum, and so prevent a bad job from becoming worse. Here, joint sclerotherapy offers an excellent chance for help.

The pain can be stopped in practically every case, but one unpleasant fact must be faced. Such a back will never be wholly well. It never was entirely healthy and, as of now, the best that routine medical science has available are a few surgical procedures of more or less doubtful value. Some are better than others. None is perfect.

Anyone afflicted in this way has to accept the fact that he's a special case, confined to a limited field as far as earning a living is concerned and with corresponding limitations on all his other activities. Obviously, nothing that involves any extra strain on the back can be considered.

To be painfully frank, if it's spondy, your back will never be perfect. The pain can certainly be stopped, and further slippage halted, but that vagrant half of the affected vertebra cannot be restored to its proper place.

A broad group of sore-back patients have what the profession calls "short leg." For once at least, the medical term covering this condition comes up in plain, unvarnished

Anglo-Saxon, and so needs no further explanation except perhaps to add that approximately eight out of every ten people are walking around with one leg longer than the other, or maybe shorter, depending on which leg you're looking at. The difference may well be undiscernible to the naked eye, and never give a bit of trouble of any kind. But if the difference in length is great enough, pain is the eventual likelihood.

This difference in leg length seldom has anything to do with outward appearances, and both the girl with legs like Miss America's and the one with legs like stovepipes can be having trouble in the same way. Only X-ray studies, made with the patient standing up, can establish the true state of affairs.

Differences of as much as three-sixteenths of an inch, about a fifteen-cent stack of nickels, are not unusual, and the difference can run up to an inch or more.

In common with spondy, short leg builds up to trouble over a long time, primarily because the condition constantly keeps the whole pelvis, including the sacroiliac, slanted to one side or the other. As a result, instead of resting on a fairly level base, the first or bottom vertebra of the spine slants to conform, while each successive vertebra above is likewise forced into an unnatural, tilted position.

Whereupon a lot of unpleasant reactions get going.

To begin with, you get a lot of unequal strains all up and down the spine with the back muscles struggling to pull your spine up straight. The crooked alignment, as any mechanic will readily understand, puts unusual wear and tear on a whole series of related joints. The nerves anywhere in the picture get jangled up.

All of which adds up to some more hurting, not to mention the fact that if it's bad enough the victim moves around like a lush with a bad list to port or starboard, as the case may be.

The Greeks called this one scoliosis, meaning a curvature,

and your doctor's fancy talk would describe the condition as scoliotic. Anybody else would probably settle for badly bent. Just by way of information, if the bending is forward, like Grandpa's, the Greeks called it lordosis, but if the curvature is out at the back, producing a humped effect, they called it kyphosis. For the present, we are considering only scoliosis, and letting lordosis and kyphosis alone.

Pretty nearly everybody has heard about one little stunt your doctor may recommend for scoliosis. He'll give you a prescription that goes to a shoemaker instead of a druggist.

By any one of several methods, the commonest being the mere tacking of an extra thickness of leather in the heel of one shoe, the leg difference can be balanced off. Perhaps, if the difference is very great, a little can be shaved off the long side while building up the other. Likewise, in extreme cases, it may be necessary to make the correction a little at a time instead of all at once.

Under ideal conditions, this procedure offers one of the most dramatic cures in the book for persistent backache, and, if you must have a bad back, you'll be happiest with one that lends itself to treatment by the shoemaker—with, of course, a good doctor calling the shots.

There's another condition which, like spondy and short leg, may have been years in the making before becoming an aching nuisance and which annually sends whole droves of patients limping to the doctor.

A while back some tricky little parts of the vertebra called articular facets were mentioned and you were warned that you'd better not lose track of them. If you've forgotten, you'd better leaf back right now and dust off your memory.

When your body is erect the principal weight above the hips rests on the forward, or body, portion of each vertebra. But the moment you bend forward from the hips, as in dishwashing at the sink or teeing off on the golf course, things change. The further forward you lean the more weight shifts off the vertebra body.

Actually, the situation is comparable to what would happen if you had a number of spools piled one on top of the other, and loosely held together by a flexible string down the center. Should this column be tilted forward, each spool would have a tendency, restrained only by the elastic center cord, to slip off the spool below.

If, in addition, a heavy downward pull were put on the upper end of the spool column, which is just about what happens to your spine when you bend from the waist to pull or lift, the spools would certainly slip off and the column would separate.

But your spine isn't a column of spools. For one thing, your spine is fitted with these articular facets.

In effect, these facets, among other very important functions, provide a series of secondary, or auxiliary, bearing surfaces so placed that they take up more and more of the weight of your upper body as you lean further and further forward. With the spine horizontal, the two downward projecting facets of an upper vertebra come to rest on two matching facets projecting upward from the vertebra immediately below. Thus a chain of overlapping bone segments is formed along the entire length of the spinal column, and the overlap helps prevent the spinal column from separating as it might otherwise do when you bend over or lift—just like the tilted column of spools.

In a vertical position, also, these facets keep each vertebra in line with its neighbors.

Any number of unhappy things can happen to these facets. In many cases, they grow in stunted, crooked, or otherwise deformed—a situation that makes more work for the doctor and no end of trouble for everybody. Anybody out to impress friends can explain that he's having trouble with a zygapophyseal joint, which ought to hold 'em awhile.

7. MORE TROUBLE

IT WOULD BE very pleasant indeed if it were possible to pass over the several rare, but important, causes of plain backache discussed in this chapter. However, there just isn't any way to avoid dealing with these five particularly dreadful diseases affecting the bones of the back. They are osteoporosis, osteomalacia, osteitis condensans, tuberculosis and cancer.

The first three attack older women more frequently than men; tuberculosis more often appears in children and young adults; while cancer of the spine follows the same pattern of incidence shown by cancer generally. Cancer is, of course, the worst of the lot, but even so, not entirely hopeless.

There is considerable doubt among physicians as to just what causes osteoporosis, which means that the bone has become more porous, less solid, and therefore weaker. It occurs with greater frequency in the lower vertebrae of women beyond the menopause or change of life.

If you're a woman of fifty, and you start having bad backache, you can start thinking about osteoporosis. If the pain seems to go deep and keep up all the time, in or out of bed, you and your doctor can think about osteoporosis some more. By this time the situations calls for an X-ray examination, especially if you can't remember any good reason, such as a fall or heavy strain, that might otherwise explain the ache.

The X-ray film will reveal the true state of affairs, and almost any technician with even limited experience can identify the characteristically indistinct, hazy reflection of the lower vertebrae indicative of osteoporosis. Fortunately, the treatment is fairly certain to bring results, despite the uncertainty as to the exact cause of the disease. The generally accepted procedure calls for periodic doses of male and female hormones, testosterone and estrogen.

Relief of pain and improvement up to positive cure, so long as the dosage is continued, have been reported. This is a long step forward, since until only a few decades ago, before the advent of modern hormone therapy, there just wasn't anything at all available by way of effective treatment.

Osteomalacia, a sort of first cousin of osteoporosis, means a softening of the bone. Actually, this disease, attacking pretty nearly any bone in the pelvis, including the lumbar vertebrae, is really a form of adult rickets, stemming from exactly the same kind of vitamin deficiency responsible for juvenile rickets.

Frequently, a diagnosis of osteomalacia in a pregnant woman will compel Caesarean delivery, because the soft, weakened bones of the pelvic outlet, through which the baby must pass, may have been deformed, twisted, shifted, or bent so as to make normal birth passage impossible.

The pain of osteomalacia is quite similar to that of osteoporosis and, again, the certain evidence is produced by an X-ray study.

But just as an increasing understanding of the nutritional factors involved has almost eliminated rickets among children, so proper diet containing the necessary components, such as vitamin D and calcium, is indicated in osteomalacia. Since it is a diet deficiency disease, osteomalacia is comparatively rare among American women, who are generally well fed.

There is no known cure for osteitis condensans. It seems to be closely associated with pregnancy, at least to the extent that pregnancy aggravates the condition. A well-developed case can produce much greater pain than either osteoporosis or osteomalacia and, once more, the X-ray plate discloses its presence beyond all doubt.

As osteitis condensans progresses, the affected bones, ordinarily the ilia, get gradually harder and harder as more and more calcium and lime are accumulated. The bones become stonelike, lacking the normal cellular composition of healthy bone, and the condition worsens with each successive pregnancy.

In severe attacks, the doctor can only offer a painkiller of some kind—narcotics, sedatives, or the like—and advise avoidance of further childbearing. That's all.

Tuberculosis of the spine takes its principal toll among the young, striking at victims anywhere from five to twenty-five years of age. Just as tuberculosis of the lungs is a consumption, or wasting away of the lung tissue, so tuberculosis of the spine is a similar wasting away of the bony parts of the spine.

Commonly, the disease develops more frequently in the upper or lower portions of the spine rather than the middle portion. The forward portion, or body, of the vertebra slowly dissolves, allowing the spine to crumble into a disordered jumble of misshapen vertebrae.

Time was, and not too long ago, when this condition in the upper, or dorsal, vertebrae invariably resulted in the development of a pronounced hump between the shoulder blades, leaving the victim a twisted, grotesque hunchback. But modern surgery has for more than thirty years been able to avert such an outcome.

The surgical method generally used is to join firmly the damaged vertebra to those sound spinal segments above and

below by means of a graft, usually from the shin. The principle is just about the same as the idea behind the chancy
bone graft sometimes used in an attempt to fix hypermobile
sacroiliacs. Happily, this type of bone-graft operation in a
tubercular spine is almost always successful, so that the sight
of a hunchback these days is very rare.

When it comes to cancer, things are admittedly bad but
increasingly less hopeless. As with cancer anywhere at all,
your chances with cancer of the spine are enormously improved by early diagnosis. There are other factors as well
that justify a more optimistic attitude toward spinal cancer
than, for instance, cancer of the bladder.

For one thing, cancer in the spine most usually originates
in a cancer of some other organ, such as the kidney, the
breast, the uterus, or the prostate. These often respond well
to treatment, and the spinal symptoms thereafter disappear.
Cases where the disease has developed first in the spine are
rare. There are actual cases on record in which spinal cancer,
induced by a cancerous prostate, was cured.

First, the cancerous prostate was removed by standard surgical procedure, after which the bones of the spine, already
deteriorating under the impact of the disease, were exposed
to carefully calculated doses of X-ray irradiation. The patient,
minus the prostate and the cancer, survived.

Up until now we have been talking about the ache you
get when something goes wrong with your back. This ought
to tell the whole story, but there's a lot of backache you can
get when there's absolutely nothing at all wrong with your
back except bad neurological company.

These backaches, your doctor will tell you, are due to
"referred causes." Through your enormously intricate system
of nerves, every organ, bone, limb and appendage, joint,
muscle, and gland of your body, right down to the last bit of
cell tissue, is responsively linked together, more or less

directly. Except for an even dozen pairs of principal nerves running to your brain, all the rest, from the tip of your big toe to the top of your scalp, ultimately tie in with your spine.

As explained in an earlier chapter, a large part of the business of keeping you alive is carried on over these nerve circuits in a completely automatic way, without conscious thinking on your part. And a good thing, too, because otherwise you'd be obliged to direct each heart beat and every breath, sleeping or walking, by a separate act of will. It's impossible to imagine just what kind of constant, detailed brainwork it would take to keep such things as your digestion, bowels, kidneys, liver, and the like on the job if these automatic nerve functions didn't tend to them. Engineers will easily compare these functions with those of modern electronic servo-mechanisms common in present-day industrial production.

While they are primarily automatic, it is also true that your conscious thinking can and does affect the working of these nerves. You can't escape reaction to the endless stream of impressions coming to you through your senses, thoughts, memories, and emotions, and the reaction you experience must inevitably have its effect on your automatic nervous system.

For example, you may choose to direct your thinking where you shouldn't. The resulting blush will betray the indiscretion. Or the sight of a dog, let's say, hit by a speeding automobile can spoil your appetite, ruin your digestion, or force an involuntary cry to your lips. The horror, disgust, and fear produced by the sight may induce nausea and vomiting, or even leave more sensitive people unconscious in a faint.

Even without the actual experience of witnessing a painful sight, the mere picture of it created by the imagination can produce something like the same result, although to a lesser degree.

By and large, day in and day out, minute by minute, these automatic nerve networks keep things going with a minimum of fuss. The proper control centers located in your spinal cord and brain get prompt and complete information about each organ and part. At the same time, the necessary orders shoot back from the control point to the various organs.

A comparison may help. Think of the stomach, if you will, as the boilerworks of a factory. The boilerworks itself is operated by a crew of firemen and stokers, but they must work to the orders of the big boss, or superintendent, who sits in his office at the other end of the plant. The superintendent, as far as the automatic functions of your stomach are concerned, is your spinal cord.

For reasons best known to the boss, this one likes to get his reports and give his orders by means of messenger boys running back and forth between his office and the boiler works. He also insists that the messenger boys, or nerve impulses, use special passageways.

These passageways, or nerve channels, are separate. The boys scurry along with the spine's instructions to the stomach over what doctors call the efferent fibers. Meanwhile, the stomach's messages to the spine get there by way of the afferent fibers. So long as you are well, so long as the plant is running smoothly, there's no trouble.

But suppose you develop ulcers, which would be about the same as the boiler springing a leak. Right away those messenger boys running along that afferent hallway go haywire, shouting frantically and incoherently in the boss's ear, trying to tell him what's up with the works. The boss, like bosses the world over, gets mad, blows his stack, and tries to outshout everybody else. He kicks up a row in his office, and the chances are he cracks down on the shipping department. This, then, is a referred cause. It's not quite fair to the shipping department, but bosses are like that. In other words, the trouble in your stomach makes its appearance in a number of symptoms, but one of these symptoms—pain—makes itself felt not only in your stomach, but also in the muscles of your back.

As a matter of fact, pain originating in prostate trouble among men, and ovarian or uterine complaints among women, almost invariably develops in the low-back areas, though the back structure itself may be otherwise healthy and sound. Naturally, no amount of treatment of any kind applied to the back in cases of this kind can do much more than run up a bigger doctor bill.

The thing to do with referred-cause backache is to treat the prime cause.

8. OF BLONDES AND PRATFALLS

So FAR, the reader could easily suppose that backaches are largely caused by defects of one kind or another in the spine or pelvis. That's exactly right.

However, anybody with an absolutely perfect back from a structural standpoint needn't feel smug about it. What's more, such a desirable state of affairs is no guarantee at all of immunity, because the bony foundation of your back is by no means the only cause of backache. Witness referred causes.

The general muscular setup can also be something of a performer when it comes to your aching back, and that brings us to a very miserable matter called spasm. Enough is known about spasm to fill a whole book, but in this treatment we will have to cover the essentials in one chapter.

Except as a word we use for a particular purpose, spasm doesn't mean much, as such, and to say that a man is suffering from muscular spasm is just about as informative as to say he's suffering from a cough. Strictly speaking, the word spasm, as applied to a muscle, merely describes a condition in which the muscle in question becomes extremely, convulsively, and involuntarily rigid. Muscular spasm is a part of all serious injury. If you are hurt in any important way, you'll experience spasm.

Such spasm is natural and, within limits, a very fine thing indeed. Before the devil thought up doctors, muscular spasm was just about the only protective measure available to nature in her effort to offer some aid in injury.

Generalizations of any kind about anything are rightly regarded as dangerous—an axiom that applies more to medicine than to any other known science. But of the muscles in the human body, one general statement does seem possible. As a matter of fact, in order to understand spasm fully, one thing relative to muscle structure must be said without any ifs, ands, or buts.

All muscles of the body, the big ones and the small ones alike, voluntary or involuntary, have only one prime function: they contract.

Given a stimulus, whether it be the demand of the subconscious upon an involuntary muscle or a conscious, reasoned decision transmitted by the brain to a voluntary muscle, the relaxed muscle in question can make only one response. It contracts.

Without the urge set up by the unconscious or conscious demand, the muscle remains relaxed, free, loose and limber. In short, uncontracted.

The thing called spasm is nothing more than such ordinarily controlled contractions gone wild. If it strikes the muscles of the coronary artery, the one feeding the heart itself, we call it angina pectoris.

If the involuntary muscles of the gastrointestinal tract go into spasm, you've got colic, spastic colitis, enteritis, pylorospasm, cholecystalgia or any other fancy name your doctor can find for bellyache. And as soon as he can induce these muscles to loosen up and relax, you'll get rid of it.

When enough irritation of any kind hits a voluntary muscle the same spasmodic contraction results. Such spasm in the muscles of the back, usually induced by sudden over-

loads or direct, violent irritation, like a pratfall on an icy sidewalk, is a certain source of backache.

In spasm, these muscles have taken matters into their own hands. Without specific orders consciously transmitted by your brain, they've decided to stiffen up in response to a demand by nature. This spasmodic, uncontrolled contraction, undertaken in open mutiny against the supreme control of your mind, is fixed, set, and rigid. No matter what orders your brain may send down to relax, loosen up, take it easy, or whatever, the renegade muscles, firmly locked in spasm, stay put. Knotted and strained, they soon begin to hurt, and there's another first-class backache for you.

A clumsy twist while climbing a tree, or an awkward pirouette in a samba exhibition may wrench or suddenly stretch a muscle beyond its normal limit. If the wrench is severe enough, the muscle may even tear or bruise a little.

Immediately, all surrounding and nearby muscles get themselves into a sort of physiological sympathy strike with the injured tissue. They tighten up spasmodically, or, as we say, go into spasm, in an effort to protect the damaged part from further hurt. This reaction is commonly designated as splinting and, sustained too long, gives you more severe pain than the original injury.

It may or may not afford some comfort to you, if you ever have a spasmodic backache of this type, to know that technically it's only a symptom. But you'll be feeling a lot better much quicker if your doctor is smart enough to spot the underlying cause of this symptom. And that can be any one of a dozen different things.

For one thing, you can hope that the symptomatic ache is merely the result of simple overstrain of one or more of your back muscles. If it is you'll be twisting and squirming around, trying to find some position in which you don't hurt so much.

But no matter what, standing or sitting, stretched out or leaning against a bar with one foot properly elevated on the brass rail, your back hurts. It hurts in any position, and any fussing around you get into in the hope of easing the pain only makes it worse. So, assuming you've got good sense, you quit monkeying around and go to bed.

That, for the moment, is about as good an idea as any, provided it isn't overdone. The fact remains that—granted the spasm you've got is as simple as we hope it is—the sooner you get to moving, the sooner you're likely to stop hurting. You can gulp some aspirin, if you like, and turn on the old, faithful electric heating pad. After all, the electric company can use the money, and feeling warm is generally more to be desired than feeling cold.

Again, strapping of one kind or another may get the call. Right now seems to be as good a time as any to get in a few licks about adhesive tape and strapping in general, and blondes in particular. Adhesive-tape strapping, honestly, is a relic of barbarism. As a useful remedy it's something else we can give back to the Indians, or whoever. To begin with, in any case in which strapping seems desirable, the elastic bandages now available do a better job. And they are a lot easier on the patient.

For certain types of people, generally fair-skinned blondes, the application of an airtight, irritating plaster of adhesive tape, wrapped on under pressure and stuck on beyond all reasonable limits, is an almost certain invitation to disaster. The situation is even worse with redheads.

Nobody in his right mind, whether physician or patient, can subscribe to strapping after seeing the angry, inflamed blisters, often the size of a half-dollar, this deplorable procedure can induce. What happens when it becomes necessary to remove the stuff is painful even to think about. Even with the best of care and under ideal conditions, it is not unusual for large areas of skin to come off with the adhesive tape, leaving the general area raw, bleeding, and searingly painful. It becomes a fair question whether to put up with the original backache or the misery strapping entails.

Accordingly, for the record and very definitely, the authors are against adhesive-tape strapping as a therapeutic measure. No veterinarian would think of using anything but an elastic pressure bandage on a horse. So why let them use adhesive on you?

When it comes to a backache definitely traceable to spasm, your doctor has a choice, but if you want to get well in a hurry, you haven't.

And then again it could be that you're maybe one of those odd-balls to be found in every doctor's practice who prefers misery. In that case you may settle for a hypodermic shot of morphine or some other narcotic, and climb back into bed. When the dope wears off, you'll still be hurting, and the longer you stay on your back the longer it will be before the pain stops.

Otherwise, and with a little better luck, your doctor may move in on you with a needle full of a promising, nonnarcotic wonder drug from South America called curare.

Since its introduction to modern medical practice in 1938, this unique painkiller has achieved a place of prime importance among the antipain weapons in the therapeutic arsenal. It's important to your doctor and it's equally important to you as a patient, and it will be given detailed consideration in this book later on.

But for the moment, let's suppose the doctor has decided that your backache is the kind curare can fix. All that's needed is a little injection, and in a pleasantly short while you'll be virtually pain-free, relaxed, and comfortable. Furthermore, you can expect this lovely effect to last for at least twenty-four hours.

Thereafter, your physician may go to work with some scientifically correct manipulative therapy, applying his trained hands and special skills to your ailing body. What with one thing and another, by the time the soothing effect of the curare has worn off, enough natural healing has taken place to make life worth living again.

But maybe the spasm you've been having isn't quite so simple. It might possibly be the end result of some other failing, such as a ruptured disk or the like.

In that case, nature may seek to help by setting up a self-produced splint around the trouble in which the adjacent muscles are spasmodically thrown into fixed, rigid immobility.

For a time this automatic reaction to the main trouble might be very good indeed—if it weren't just too bad. If that sounds like double talk, its only because Nature, ordinarily pretty smart, here doesn't seem to make much sense from a practical standpoint.

It's like this.

If the kind of trouble we are now considering were to happen to some happy savage, far removed from the sometimes dubious advantages of modern medical science, this natural splinting could serve an extremely useful function. It would certainly force the patient to accept the only course available to him in his medical ignorance—rest and immobility. What's more, the enforced inaction might even result in a cure in due time. Most doctors will hasten to explain that such cases are rare, but rare or not, they can turn up.

Actually, few people would want to endure voluntarily the protracted misery they'd have to endure while waiting for an unassisted natural cure. Moreover, for better or worse, we are no longer carefree children of the jungles either, and so we've come to expect our physicians to give Nature a little help.

This being the case, the best strategy in sight when it's a matter of splinting induced by injury, and not the result of simple strain, is to treat the injury itself. Certainly the splinting itself will constitute a source of pain aside from anything else, especially if it has been going on for any prolonged stretch of time.

But—and this is of prime importance—the most careful diagnosis must be made to determine clearly whether or not your muscle spasm is due to strain, or the result of injury.

It's important because it will do you no good at all, and will probably do a lot of harm, to relieve or relax the tension if something other than simple strain is causing it. Such a procedure might admittedly give a most welcome easing of pain, but unless the underlying cause is corrected, your freedom from pain would merely permit you to engage in greater activity than you should, thereby doing still further damage.

On the other hand, if your splinting is definitely the result of a sudden overstrain, a bad twist or a fall, and no other damage is involved, you're a lucky fellow indeed and your doctor should have just the thing for you. You'll get a shot in the arm, or in the slats, or anywhere you prefer, and in less than an hour you'll be on your way rejoicing.

As often as not, one shot will do it. If not, a second dose the next day will, and that will be that. The whole treatment requires nothing further. No strapping, no pain-pills, no diathermy, and a minimum expenditure of time and money.

Should something more serious turn up, other measures, more extensive as well as more expensive, will have to be applied. It could be that you and your doctor are up against either a bad disk or a slipped sacroiliac, or any one of several other and more complicated conditions.

For example, there's the mishap that sometimes occurs in certain more vulnerable spines whereby those pesky articular facets of the vertebra literally get themselves into a jam. Instead of sliding across each other smoothly and easily as they should, they get stuck at some point in their passage.

Pretty nearly everybody, at one time or another, has had to listen politely while a friend goes into a lot of tiresome detail about how all he did was to reach down to pick up his shoes one morning, or perform some equally innocent bending motion, and bang—there it was.

In all likelihood, what happened was that somewhere along his spine a set of these articular facets, probably those of the fourth and fifth lumbar vertebrae, got into a tight bind as he straightened up. They've stuck on one side or the other, or possibly both sides, and so they've twisted the vertebra out of its proper position. Doctors call this a subluxation. Needless to say, it hurts.

The condition may produce some attendant splinting, and then again maybe it won't, all of which doesn't matter because there's only one proper course of treatment worth considering anyhow.

The jammed facets will have to be unjammed somehow, usually by the application of carefully calculated pressures to various parts of the body which, using natural leverage and taking advantage of the normal functions of all related factors, will cause these displaced parts to resume their proper place. In medicine this procedure is known as manipulative therapy.

Finally, another affliction of the back is fibrositis.

There's no use trying to kid anybody about fibrositis, either, because when it's all said and done, nobody knows exactly what it is. Doctors can, to be sure, explain that fibrositis is "the syndrome of pain, stiffness or aching appearing in any portion of the fibrous tissue about bones and joint." By this it would appear that fibrositis is a pain, and this will come as no surprise to anyone who has it.

For one thing, fibrositis is a chronic condition. It shows up painfully just from sitting too long in one place. It's at its worst first thing in the morning, and shows a tendency to ease off as the day wears on.

The doctor's probing fingers may encounter a certain lumpiness and unnatural rigidity in the low-back muscles.

It's almost certain that somebody will mention arthritis, assuming that the patient hasn't thought of it himself. It's usual too, to find that diathermy, trick injections, and therapeutic corsets, with or without laces and garter supports or both, are in the picture. They almost always ought to be out of it.

There are, of course, better methods of dealing with fibrositis, even if nobody knows what they are. For the moment it will serve merely to suggest that fibrositis sufferers make sure to dress warmly in cold weather. Warmly means woolen underwear, socks and mittens. Better yet—red flannels, supposing fibrositis is worse than wounded vanity.

9. WHAT'S THE MATTER WITH YOU?

WHEN ALL is said and done, you are the diagnostician; your aching back makes the diagnosis.

What you tell your doctor in answer to his questions, the results of whatever tests he may recommend, and a number of other considerations get into the picture sooner or later. To a considerable degree, the more accurately you can describe your condition, and the more plainly you can answer his questions, the more likely it is that you'll get well.

The inability of most patients to explain clearly what ails them is a long-standing source of dismay to modern medicine, and the reason why so many physicians prefer to specialize in pediatrics. At least their child patients can't confuse matters with any adult symptomatic baloney acquired from reading patent-medicine ads. That helps a lot.

It may be hard to believe, but the fact remains that there's an awful pile of doctoring being done on backache in which neither the doctor, the patient, nor the cop on the corner has the faintest notion of just exactly what's wrong. Often, and too often, the patient simply reports a pain in the back, and the doctor just as simply offers a little diathermy, a bit of adhesive-tape strapping, or maybe even some heavy dosage of a wonder drug called acetylsalicylic acid (aspirin), administered orally.

All of which is just so much nonsense. It's bad enough that foolishness of this kind can cost the sufferer both time and money, not to mention hours and days of pain. Worse, the delay in coming round to proper and adequate treatment can lead to permanent harm, which might otherwise have been averted.

The good chances are that you are reading this because you have a bad back yourself, or someone you care about has one. Our objective is to help you help yourself. So let's consider your case.

If he's the kind of a doctor you ought to have, your doctor will bless you if you have thought out the answers to some things he'll want to know beforehand. If he isn't, the diagnosis won't matter because no matter what your trouble may be, you'll get either diathermy, strapping, or the aforementioned wonder drug—or, if things are grave, all three at once.

Consideration of your case begins with what the doctor calls a history, which means anything and everything you can tell about your situation from the very beginning. And with every fact you give him, your true diagnosis becomes more evident. With enough facts, your diagnosis becomes unmistakable. Accurate diagnosis is as much, if not more, a matter of determining what you haven't got. It is basically a process of elimination.

For one thing, no one knows how many deluded, misinformed, and unhappy folks are limping around with nonexistent arthritis. Time and time again they turn up to offer histories in which they relate how Dr. So-and-So has traced the agony to arthritis. With no laboratory examination, no X-ray study, no judgment, and no brains, some doctor has pronounced their doom out of hand and entirely wrong.

Make no mistake. True arthritis of the vertebral joints in the spine, or the pelvic joints of the sacroiliac, is a dreadful and practically incurable disease. Worse yet, its earliest symptoms, primarily backache, are generally the same as those of several other more prevalent back disorders.

But—and this is most important—unless there have been X-ray studies, plus certain well-established laboratory tests, don't let anybody tell you you have arthritis. There are any number of physicians, all qualified back specialists, who have been practicing for years and seeing patients day in and day out, who have yet to encounter a single case of genuine arthritis. The thought of many unfortunates, hopelessly and needlessly living under a false sentence of arthritis is tragically painful.

Sight unseen, pending the X-ray study, we assume you don't have arthritis.

With arthritis out of the picture, the most likely possibilities are acute low-back strain, a bad disk, or fibrositis, in that order, and to some extent each displays one or more characteristics easily identified by the patient alone. You can pretty nearly check yourself on these three.

For instance, if your backache is one that usually nags away at a fairly constant nuisance level until a move of some sort gives you a real wallop, worth anything from a grunt to a yell, you've no doubt got an acute low-back strain. A symptom of this sort likewise pretty well rules out either fibrositis or disk.

Again, your backache may shoot down one leg or the other, or even both. If it does, you can be fairly certain you've got disk trouble, and just as sure that there's no fibrositis or low-back strain.

As to fibrositis, the indications are also pretty clear. If that's your trouble, you can't help noticing that it's worse in the morning. You wake up with your backache. It's not what you'd call a killing pain, but nevertheless it hurts, and bending over to tie the shoelaces is a tough job. Straightening up again is tougher.

The only good thing about it is the certainty that in an hour or two you'll limber up a little and, provided you keep moving around, the pain will be gone at least until tomorrow morning. But sitting still for moderately long periods will surely kick up the fuss in your back again. That's fibrositis.

With any painful ailment on the books, accurate diagnosis comes close to being all important as far as ultimate cure is concerned. But even so, the diagnosis you yourself make with every groan is all too often enough to warrant immediate treatment designed to allay the pain, and both you and your doctor can be forgiven if the long-range view is ignored for the time being.

When you limp into his office, let's hope your doctor is enough of a realist, not to mention humanitarian, to set theoretical diagnosis aside long enough to give you a working dose of any one of the highly effective painkillers presently in use. On the other hand, he may be the kind who will rise

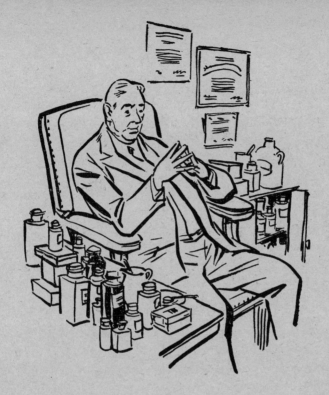

heroically above any immediate consideration of your pain during the week or so he may need for your first, or tentative, diagnosis.

Then again, your doctor may be of a different variety, leaning to excessive doses of painkiller, diathermy, routine strapping, or the like. In the first instance, all you're getting is a lot of diagnosis and no treatment, while in the second you're getting the same thing, reading from right to left and reverse.

The thing for you, in either case, is to get as far away from there as fast as your aching back will let you—and stay away until you have found a doctor with good sense.

Such a doctor will be fully aware that any leg pain you may note, whether in one leg or both, is in all probability the result of a bad disk. People call it sciatica, which merely means that the big sciatic nerve running down the back of each leg is inflamed. Certainly, neither low-back strain nor fibrositis, operating independently, can cause sciatica.

Broadly speaking, accurate diagnosis of practically any back condition, except low-back strain, is virtually impossible without careful X-ray studies. In particular, disk problems and spondylolisthesis (spondy), present much the same symptomatic picture, as previously noted. In the absence of X-ray studies, nobody, least of all a reputable doctor, would stick out his neck far enough to name either one.

But for the rest, in sacroiliac slips and just about all other backaches arising from structural disorders of the spine and pelvis, X rays are normally valuable, but further investigation is often necessary to establish the cause of the trouble beyond reasonable doubt.

For a complete X-ray study of the back, at least five and possibly seven separate views should be taken. Two are the absolute minimum. A single shot aimed right through the middle, for example, serves no useful purpose at all. The whole gallery shouldn't cost over fifty dollars.

Excessive exposure to X rays is certainly dangerous. In particular, indiscriminate X-ray surveys of pregnant women may harm the unborn child. Accordingly, X-ray studies should be made only when clearly necessary. Carried out under the direction of a competent physician, such carefully considered X-ray examination is entirely safe.

Beyond the X-ray sittings, a few laboratory tests are sometimes indicated. One such, called a blood uric acid determination, currently priced at around five dollars, may spot some metabolic or organic disorder lurking behind your aching back. Another pair of exams, running to about twenty dollars a set, are called serum alkaline and serum acid phosphatase. They are for men only, and may trace the pain to a cancerous prostate.

Finally, a basal metabolism job, cheap at about twenty-five dollars, might unmask some thyroid condition as the real villain.

· When all possibilities have been added up, you'll qualify for treatment under one or more headings. So it's time to treat.

10. A WINNING HAND

For specific types of backache cases, three remarkable and uniformly effective therapies now in current use must command the attention of both physicians and patients, for they are truly major milestones in humanity's pain-shadowed pathway to a healthier, happier existence.

They are manipulation, sclerotherapy, and curare. We shall consider each of these separately and in that order.

Manipulation, meaning nothing more than the scientific and restful application of gentle hands to make the most of the curative powers inherent in them, is easily the most direct, simple, and natural therapy known to mankind.

Certainly manipulation of one kind or another has been an instinctive remedy for musculoskeletal disorders for a very long time—something on the order of a million years, which is one informed guess as to just how long human beings have been around. But the refined and highly developed manipulative techniques practiced today were devised not much more than eighty years ago, and the field is still under exploration.

It's safe to assume that the first caveman who ever cracked his low-browed head against the ceiling of the family residence just naturally rubbed the ensuing bump. Perhaps he

banged his knee, or worse yet, a shinbone on a rock while scrambling away from an irritated dinosaur. He rubbed those bruises too.

The most ignorant savage and the cultured college dean alike will hug their tummy with a bellyache, press a soothing hand against an aching brow. You rub your frost-nipped ears or nose, and your hands too. All such rubbing, pressing, stroking, smoothing is natural, and it's manipulation, whether practiced by a physician or a Hottentot.

For centuries, in certain parts of Europe a back-weary peasant would plod home to his cottage at eventide and detail one of the younger children to provide relief for him by walking around barefooted on his bare back. This too is essentially manipulation.

Such instinctive therapy, refined, organized, and scientifically applied by a skilled physician, is the payoff answer to a whole list of backaches, beginning with our old devil, the classic sacroiliac slip. Men like Dr. Joel Goldthwaite of Boston City Hospital, the former president of the American Orthopedic Association and others have used such manipulative techniques. Dr. Still is, of course, the recognized originator of these scientific manipulative procedures.

Manipulation is used to soothe jangled nerves, ease rigid muscles and cramped joints, set broken bones, adjust dislocations, and stimulate circulation, thereby easing the work load your heart must carry.

By its use, your doctor can get you three very important results. For one thing, he can step up your blood circulation. For another, he can relax painful muscles in your back and pretty nearly anywhere else. Finally, he can put certain kinds of joint disorders to rights. All three are big factors in your recovery from what ails you, but blood circulation is in all probability the one that matters most, if only because improvement here has an effect on the body as a whole.

Here's why.

Any kind of healing, from that of a simple pimple to virus X, depends finally on circulation. Your blood stream is literally the River of Life as far as you're concerned. It has the lifelong job of hauling nutrition and energy to all parts of your body and carrying off the worn-out, waste tissue cells it picks up around the circuit.

The way this works has been well known ever since a writing fellow named Will Shakespeare was pub crawling around London. About the same time there was another famous William in England whose last name was Harvey. He was a doctor at St. Bartholomew's Hospital, destined to settle all previous odd notions about the circulatory system once and for all with a famous treatise called "Anatomical Study of the Movement of the Heart and the Blood." What Harvey said then, with a few additions and no corrections, still goes.

The basic drive of your blood stream comes from that

mighty little pumper, the heart. Sleeping or waking, in active motion or when you are at ease, your heart keeps your share of the world's blood supply, about five quarts for an adult, on its all-important circuit of arteries and veins.

This pumping function of the heart is well known, but what isn't generally as well understood is the fact that the heart gets appreciable help in its work from other organs and parts of the body not directly devoted to maintaining blood pressure.

When your doctor wraps that rubber bandage around your arm and pumps up on the little rubber bulb, he's getting a line on your blood pressure, and the gadget he's using is a sphygmomanometer. If you can pronounce it, you're probably in good shape anyhow. The sphygmomanometer will give the doctor two readings on the calibrated scale that is part of the device. The high reading, running anywhere from 100 to 300 or more, is made by the spurt of blood surging through your arteries as your heart contracts.

This is the systolic pressure.

In between each spurt, or beat, there's a low point, registering a normal range from about 60 to 90. This is the diastolic pressure.

The average, unexcited, mature male, who isn't mad at anybody, worried about anything, or afraid of something, will run a sphygmomanometer reading of about 130 over 80, give or take a few points.

Neither your sex, your politics, nor the shape of your ears —much less your age—has anything at all to do with these figures, regardless of what your smart friend may tell you about how your blood pressure should be "100 plus your age," or some such nonsense.

But exertion of any kind, or strong emotional excitement such as undue reaction to certain females, can whip up your blood pressure, jazz up your pulse, hop up your respiration,

A.
PALMS UP·
ARMS EXTENDED
STRAIGHT OUT

B.
MAKE FISTS·
TIGHTEN
MUSCLES

C.
SWING FISTS
CLOSE AS POSSIBLE
TO SHOULDERS

D.
WHIP ARMS
OUT STRAIGHT
AGAIN

and foul up a lot of things, all of them dependent on your blood stream.

Getting back to your heart, and the help it gets from other parts of the body like your diaphragm, legs, arms, and maybe even your jaws, try this: Stick your arm straight out in front of you, palm up, and then make a fist. Then, with the arm muscles tightened, bend the elbow to bring the fist up as close as possible to the shoulder, pressing hard. Then whip the arm out straight again.

Very plainly, you've squeezed the blood out of some parts of the arm like the lower biceps, forcing it along the surrounding veins and arteries. Similar pressures, set up for instance in the legs when you stoop or squat to thin out the petunias in the garden, have the same general effect. It is this alternate tightening and loosening of your muscles as you move about, intermittently squeezing the blood out of the tissue, that sets up a secondary but valuable pumping action, cutting down the work load on the heart.

So also, the regular expansion and contraction of the chest as you inhale and exhale, and the powerful, rhythmic thrust of your diaphragm, provide more extra pumping power. Even the mere swing of your legs and arms in walking helps.

Muscle movement of this kind, or any body motion in general, breathing included, works somewhat like the booster pumps that engineers install at intervals on long oil transmission lines like the "Big Inch." They furnish auxiliary pumping power.

Therapeutic manipulation, in effect, merely supplements the extra pumping help your heart gets from these boosters by external pressures applied at strategic spots. Such supplementary help costs the patient no strain because the doctor puts up all the effort. As a result, the circulation becomes full, steady, and strong, revitalizing and refreshing the entire body.

As a further result, the patient feels better, which is what he came to the doctor for in the first place.

Such general improvement, possible through proper manipulation by a well-trained physician, is worth the price of admission even in the absence of any specific complaint, just for the sake of general well-being, and without reference to any particular malaise.

An otherwise relaxed and comfortable patient is in much better shape to deal with pretty nearly any localized symptom or pain he may have—a toothache or a hang-over, let's say— simply because good circulation is a basic requirement to feeling good.

No matter what kind of a crick you may get in your back, whether caused by a failing disk, some pelvic or sacroiliac maladjustment, fibrositis, spondy, or whatever, you're going to respond in two ways. First, you'll feel pain. Second, you'll develop a lot of what the doctor calls muscle spasm.

By spasm, as we have said, the doctor means the rigid stiffness, amounting almost to paralysis, that strikes the muscles in the vicinity of your trouble. Tensely locked in an auto-

matic contraction, the muscles have instinctively set themselves against possible motion.

The end result is an additional ache, superimposed on the
initial pain. The discomfort produced by spasm is exactly
like the muscle soreness you get any time you go in for unusual activity of any kind—a strenuous game of tennis or golf
after a long winter of vigorous TV viewing, perhaps. This
soreness is not an injury, to be sure, and nothing that some
rest or some smart manipulation oughtn't to fix easily.

But a muscle in spasm, hurting in exactly the same way,
gets no rest so long as the original irritation responsible for
the spasm continues, and that makes for a chain reaction of
trouble in which the more pain you have, the more pain you
get. And you can expect the pain to keep right on for as long
as it takes you to get some sensible treatment for it.

Until then, you are the star of a physiological tearjerker.
The plot goes something like this: First, something goes
wrong in your back causing pain. Second, the affected muscles go into spasm, thereby causing more pain. Third, the
painful spasm retards circulation, which deprives the spasm-
locked, pain-ridden muscles of their best blood supply just
when they need it most. Fourth, the spasm-locked, pain-
ridden, blood-starved muscles begin to deteriorate. They lose
their tone and vitality, developing stiff, fibrous tissues instead
of supple, sound muscle-stuff. Fifth, this degeneration of the
cells causes pain. So the spasm-locked, pain-ridden, blood-

starved, cell-deteriorated back muscles go into spasm, and that's where we came in, and anybody who wants to sit in on the second show is welcome to the seat.

Long before this merry-go-round gets into high gear, the more sensible doctors will be applying soothing pressure and scientific, external, manual adjustment. The spasm-torn muscles, relaxed and relieved, will stop hurting, the blood supply will return to normal, and the way will be cleared for a direct approach to the initial irritation.

Except in advanced cases of disk rupture, where manipulation may only make matters worse, skilled manipulation can alleviate a considerable number of backaches in short order.

But even beyond improvement of the circulation or relief of muscle spasm, manipulative techniques are increasingly the treatment of choice among progressive physicians everywhere for the common sacroiliac slip.

There's no need to repeat what has already been said relative to manipulation of sacroiliac slips in the earlier chapter, because the situation hasn't changed a bit since then.

Furthermore, the treatment itself needn't be in any way painful, even though the condition may call for a major correction of a very old and deeply rooted complaint accompanied by great pain. Such manipulative therapies can be performed under a simple anesthesia just as well, and in many instances even better. Often enough, here is another welcome escape hatch for some backache victims whose only alternative may be painful, expensive surgery.

Reporting on observed disk cases, Dr. Merrill C. Mensor, in the October, 1955, *Journal of Bone and Joint Surgery,* said in part, "In this series, complete symptomatic relief occurred considerably more often after manipulation and the accompanying conservative regimen than after surgical therapy. . . ."

And from all indications, manipulation will continue to be the best way to handle sacroiliac slip, as well as for any needed adjustment of the lumbar vertebra, for a very long time to come. Experience has proved the curative value of this kind of therapy beyond all question.

Nor is it at all new, it appears. Hippocrates, the head doctor in ancient Greece, was using comparable techniques a good twenty-three hundred years ago. As Hippocrates put it, in the book he wrote for student doctors of the day, manipulation "can relax, brace, incarnate, attenuate: hard braces, soft relaxes, much attenuates, and moderate thickens."

In other words, manipulation is a very fine thing.

11. SCLEROTHERAPY, A NEW DEAL

BESIDES ADVANCED manipulation, another relatively new procedure based on a remedial technique as old as medicine itself promises soon to revolutionize many therapeutic standbys, starting with the management of the ruptured disk.

This is joint sclerotherapy.

In addition to disk problems, such instabilities as the common "trick knee" of football players, recurrent shoulder dislocations and sacroiliac problems, as well as structural failures of all kinds, are being increasingly met by sclerotherapy.

As a therapeutic technique, sclerotherapy represents the latest forward step in the never-ending war on certain human miseries, as well as a modern application of ancient healing wisdom.

This time, the Greeks not only provide the word, but to a very large degree, the prototype treatment.

In sclerotherapy, scar tissue, nature's own response to a whole series of difficulties, is used to produce cures not otherwise possible without extensive, ordinarily expensive surgery.

Scars as such have seldom been welcomed, usually concealed, and generally lamented, except for the honorable scars of battle proudly worn by fighting men since ancient times. German university students of a bygone day eagerly

sought such scars, deep creases in the cheek or forehead, in bloody saber duels with fellow students.

Pits and scars observed on the faces and bodies of small-pox victims played a large part in Edward Jenner's revolutionary discovery of vaccination, and the scar on your left arm is nothing more than some scarified tissue caused by the cowpox they gave you to ward off the smallpox that might have killed you.

A strip-tease artist, for instance, naturally isn't going to regard the results of her appendectomy or panhystorectomy as an asset in her work, and the chances are good that the customers will agree with her. Nor is there any point in for-

100

getting that disfiguring facial scars have ruined countless lives, except where plastic surgery has been able to help.

But even so, scar tissue often plays an important part in natural healing, aiding in recoveries not otherwise possible. Let's consider for instance what would happen in severe burns where the skin-producing cells have been destroyed beyond all repair. Without the development of scar tissue as an admittedly inferior, but nevertheless effective substitute, such burns would almost certainly all prove fatal.

Likewise, without the ultimate development of scar tissue to close incisions permanently, no surgery of any kind would be possible. The stitches first used can't possibly do more than hold the edges of the surgical incision in place until natural scar tissue can knit them together once more. Then the sutures are either removed, or, if not accessible after deep surgery, permitted to dissolve.

The role of scar tissue in repairing wounds of all kinds has been known to mankind since earliest times. Superstitious awe of the accidentally acquired scars of battle and the chase often led to deliberate religious scarification, practiced by many savage tribes since time immemorial. As an aid to physicians in treating their patients for certain ailments, artificially induced scars are even older.

As a matter of record, more than two thousand years ago Hippocrates was performing an operation on recurrent shoulder dislocations in which the objective was to produce heavy scars in the armpit, thereby keeping the shoulder from slipping out of its socket all the time. His description of this operation still sounds like pretty good doctoring, considering the fact that he was starting from scratch.

"It deserves to be known," he wrote, "how a shoulder which is subject to frequent dislocations should be treated." Lots of lads, he went on, had to quit gymnasium pastimes like boxing and wrestling on account of such tricky shoulders, and some of them even were killed in battle because their sword arms quit at the wrong time.

"I have never known any physician to treat the case properly," the old pro grumbled. Furthermore, some of his fellow doctors "abandon the attempt altogether" while others "practice the very reverse of what is proper."

The proper technique for his time, Hippocrates goes on to explain, is to raise the patient's arm about halfway up and make a couple of quick vertical cuts in the armpit with a red-hot cautery. "The cauteries should be red-hot," he cautions, "that they may pass through as quickly as possible."

The ensuing scars would provide the necessary support to keep the shoulder from dislocation, Hippocrates declared. This then, was the earliest example of sclerotherapy—otherwise, treatment by scarring. It's come a long way since.

Through the centuries, such rudimentary sclerotherapy, like countless other surgical and medical ideas, passed into the general body of therapeutic resources available to physicians as they chose.

Something more than one hundred years ago, a French doctor named Valpeau was feeling his way into a sclerotherapeutic method in which he was shooting hypodermic injections of iodine into patients suffering from abdominal ruptures. If the iodine could start the growth of scar tissue to provide support for the rupture, he figured, there might not be any need for the crude, cumbersome trusses then in use. Sometimes, he found out, his novel idea worked.

By the early 1930's, Dr. I. William Lippman, associate in urology at Bronx Hospital in New York, following years of study, was able to declare such procedures a success in the treatment of hernia.

"The closure of hernial rings could be accomplished by the injection of a solution capable of producing fibrous tissue," Dr. Lippman reported. "Such treatment," he added, "will take its place beside many other outstanding advances in the healing art."

A few years later, in 1937, sclerotherapy was extended to a new and entirely different type of case. At the general clinic of the Osteopathic Hospital in Philadelphia, Dr. Earl Gedney, presently a staff surgeon at Riverview Hospital in Norristown, began to report remarkable results from the application of a sclerotherapy technique to weakened, wobbly knee joints once dealt with by braces or operations.

Soon he was joined by Dr. David Shuman, co-author of this book, then an examiner at the clinic and an instructor at the Philadelphia College of Osteopathy.

To both Gedney and Shuman the customary operation, requiring removal of supposedly useless though healthy cartilage from the knee, just didn't make sense. Just because this cartilage may have slipped out of place was no reason, they figured, for cutting it out altogether. The structurally weakened ligaments linking the various parts of the knee needed stiffening.

Strengthen these, they argued, and the knee joint would remain properly in place without braces and without operation. Some scar tissue developed in the ligaments by injection of a sclerosing solution would provide needed toughness in the same way as Dr. Lippman reinforced the hernia tissues affected by rupture.

The next step, application of sclerotherapy to weakened sacroiliacs, was easy. No operation, no blood, no bone grafts. Just a little weekly hypodermic injection, repeated ten or perhaps a dozen times, and the sacroiliac stayed put.

But when it came to problems like spondy, beyond the reach of all operative techniques, and ruptured disks, where operations could promise only a little more than half a chance at complete recovery, sclerotherapy assumed its greatest significance. No myelograms, no nucleograms, no arthrodesis, no fusions, not even hospitalization. Just simple injections, easily given at an office visit the patient could make on his way to the movies.

A recent review in the *Journal of the American Medical Association* best summarizes the progress of joint sclerotherapy since Gedney and Shuman first began their work.

The report, written for the *Ohio State Medical Journal* on "Joint Stabilization Through Induced Ligament Sclerosis" by Dr. G. S. Hackett, was based on scores of cases, the *Journal* pointed out. Fully 82 per cent, he announced, were helped, with the relief lasting in some cases for as long as fourteen years.

What Dr. Hackett had to say about sclerotherapy soon got official recognition from the American Medical Association.

On January 9, 1954, the Association published Dr. Hackett's results.

In the fourteen years between 1939 and 1953 the *Journal* reported, Dr. Hackett applied sclerotherapy in 253 cases of sacroiliac trouble, and, the report continued, an exceptional percentage got better.

Dr. Hackett reported a few even more significant observations. "Relaxation of the sacroiliac ligaments is an important factor in low-back pain," he declared. What he meant was that, except for pregnancy cases, a lot of curable low-back pain, cricks, aches, twinges and general hurting was traceable to a loosening or softening or, in medical language, relaxation of the sacroiliac ligaments tying the bones of the sacroiliac and, in turn, the whole pelvis, together.

When that happens, Dr. Hackett said, the sacroiliac, deprived of regular support, would slip, resulting in what a doctor would call an unstable joint. The patient would call it a backache.

Here, Dr. Hackett reported, the old diagnostic standby, X rays, didn't help much. To be sure, the Chamberlain test for sacroiliac mobility would spot the trouble in an advanced stage, but there was a better way, Dr. Hackett found.

If an anesthetic injection into the sacroiliac, such as procaine, could alleviate the immediate agony, the chances were better than good that strengthening the ligaments was the answer. So Dr. Hackett shot doses of sclerosing solution into the faulty ligaments. Soon heavy, tough scars developed. Stiffened by the scars, the ligaments once more became strong enough to support the joint.

In short, the patient got well.

The results obtained by Drs. Hackett, Gedney, and Shuman, to name a few, firmly established the new technique as an acceptable and increasingly desirable alternative to the older operative procedures.

Such artificially induced scar tissue at predetermined and easily located points provides the extra strength needed by a loose, wobbly sacroiliac, for instance. The same technique can stiffen the flabby, misshapen ligaments of a collapsed

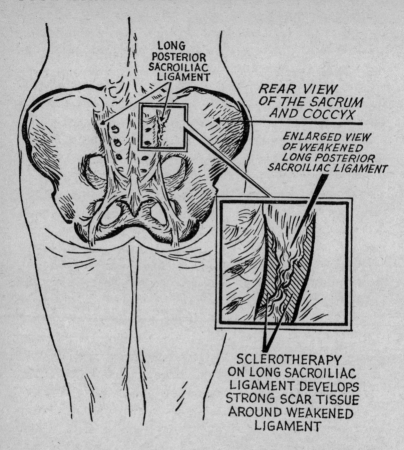

LONG
POSTERIOR
SACROILIAC
LIGAMENT

*REAR VIEW
OF THE SACRUM
AND COCCYX*

ENLARGED VIEW
OF WEAKENED
LONG POSTERIOR
SACROILIAC LIGAMENT

SCLEROTHERAPY
ON LONG SACROILIAC
LIGAMENT DEVELOPS
STRONG SCAR TISSUE
AROUND WEAKENED
LIGAMENT

disk. It can brace vertebrae where poorly developed facets fail to function properly, and it can halt the relentless forward slip of the lumbar vertebrae characteristic of spondylolisthesis.

For spondy, sclerotherapy is the only known remedial method presently available, other than the dubious belts, braces, and the like. Ever since the Royal College of Surgeons called a halt on further surgical explorations, surgery as such has been entirely out of the picture in cases of this type.

For spondylolisthesis, no matter how severe the case, sclerotherapy can be truly a godsend. It offers a chance, and a very good chance at that, to escape the admitted hazards of standard operative measures.

With virtually no risk at all, at only a fraction of the cost in time and money, these major spinal and pelvic disorders can almost certainly be helped, and frequently cured.

A few examples, taken from among hundreds on file, are interesting.

As given in the phraseology peculiar to medical reports, this one begins: "Case 2: June 27th, 1950; N.R., white, male, age 32."

This "white, male, age 32" earned his living driving a tractor, and he'd been having back trouble ever since he was sixteen. As far as he could tell, he was having back trouble for no reason at all. He hadn't fallen, or been bumped, or anything like it.

But, he reported, his back got bad enough for surgery; so when he was twenty there was an operation in which the disk, the one between the big lumbar vertebra at the bottom of the spine and the first sacral vertebra immediately below, was removed. Or, as the surgeons say, "resected."

The young man got along fairly well for a few years afterward, but by the time he was twenty-seven, in 1945, he was back on the table for some more surgery. This time the operation removed some adjacent ligaments around the spot where previously they'd removed the disk. And while they were about it, the disk between the fifth lumbar vertebra and the fourth, or next above, was removed for good measure.

With the disks both above and below the vertebra gone, the man went along for all of three years. In 1948 he turned up again to complain of a bad pain in his left leg.

This time the examination located the trouble in his

sacroiliac, for a change, and also for a change there was no operation.

Instead, he got sclerotherapy, and a lot of relief. But although his sacroiliac was once more in fine shape, the man still had his backache, which was just what he started with two operations and long years back.

And except for sclerotherapy, he could still be having his backache.

Faced with continuing pain even after removal of the disks, and with the sacroiliac situation eliminated as a possibility by sclerotherapy, the spotlight moved back to the spine. Sure enough, the disks were safely out. The patient couldn't be getting pain from distorted disk pressure, as was supposed, any more than a tooth can ache after it's pulled.

But some more tests showed the diskless fourth vertebra was obviously shifting around and still raising Cain despite the two operations. The joint, in medical terminology, was unstable. The condition was ideal for sclerotherapy, and when it was carried out the results were ideal, too.

In 1950, the former patient wrote his doctor a letter. "I am feeling fine," he wrote, "and I've been driving the tractor for three weeks . . . improving every day. . . . My back feels stronger than ever."

For A. McK., a 35-year-old government arsenal employee, sclerotherapy spelled the difference between losing a job and having one, not to mention getting rid of the pain that had been dogging him for fourteen years. Maybe Uncle Sam got a break, too, because McK. was a key man at the arsenal in planning the Army's latest atomic field-piece. He was not indispensable, of course, but rather another one of those thousands of government workers, each of whom holds a corner, however tiny, of the latest Big Secret, and is therefore hard to replace.

The attacks began easy and built up. A day lost here, later

another week off, and no relief. There were visits to first one doctor, then another.

Three days of agony in a row sent him at last to a doctor who came up with a diagnosis of spondylolisthesis, the grimly inexorable vertebral slippage before which regular surgery, with its scalpels and chisels, saws and hammers, anaesthesia and sutures, was helpless.

Nobody told the patient about those two unfortunate Britishers who had died long ago in that desperate attempt to develop a specific operation for spondylolisthesis. But a ban laid down by the Royal College of Surgeons is likely to dominate surgical practice the civilized world over.

Nor was there any pessimistic advice like, "You'll just have to learn to live with it," or talk of "limitations." No belt or harness, either.

Instead, treatment, consisting of a simple hypodermic injection right in the doctor's office, was begun at once. Thirteen shots and sixteen weeks later, McK. stopped showing up for treatment, for the very good reason that he had no more pain.

More than a year after his last treatment, they checked up on McK. "I'm still on the job," he announced, "and feeling fine."

Then there's the young woman who tumbled out of her saddle while horseback riding at age fifteen. She came to the doctor's office nine years later, a year after her wedding. Soon after she fell off the horse, her back had started hurting from time to time, but nothing was ever done about it.

By the time she got around to it, her back was giving her so much trouble she was deliberately avoiding motherhood for fear that she just couldn't endure childbirth in addition to the pain of her aching back.

Neither she nor her husband were at all pleased with the idea of passing up having a family. On a Chamberlain test,

she showed up with what was plainly a hypermobile sacro-iliac resulting from the fall from horseback.

To make a long story into a happy ending, she got sclerotherapy. After fourteen more trips to the doctor's office she was well. Less than a year after that, she had a bouncing baby girl.

Or take the man who worked as a guard in a public museum, where his job kept him on his feet all day until a collapsed disk put him into a hospital for the standard operation. They opened up his back, cut away an intervening portion of the vertebra and scraped out the wreckage of the damaged disk. Then they sewed him up.

That was in March. By the following June, the man was down again with pains as bad or even worse than before the operation.

His morale was low, his financial resources lower, and his hopes of getting anywhere were lower yet. In less than three months and with exactly eleven treatments, sclerotherapy

had him back on the job dusting off the statues and directing visitors to the appropriate washrooms.

These little tales from the files make no pretense at offering any statistical picture, and a complete case-by-case survey of the results obtained by sclerotherapy has yet to be made. But even without one, there is far and away enough favorable evidence in hand to warrant a long look by all concerned, and an even longer look by patients facing old-fashioned, expensive, and needless surgery.

As can well be expected, there is presently no lack of melancholy statistics attesting to the widespread incidence of backache. It's an affliction to be found wherever there are backs.

Medical doctors from down-under Australia right around the globe to Alaska, and from Brooklyn to Whitechapel, reporting in the venerable *Journal of Bone and Joint Surgery*, have compiled a few statistical enumerations, though nothing like a comprehensive roundup. The *Journal* is the orthopedic bible of physicians the world over, and the figures presented, even while not complete, are at least as impressive as the hearty moans of anguish coming from whole armies of backache patients roosting in doctors' offices day in and day out.

The mere numbers of our fellow citizens laid low by herniated disks alone add up to a sum total of mass misery, so great that nobody yet has been willing to undertake the job of making a definite count. But some very startling figures are nevertheless available, notably in the records of the Medical Service Association of Pennsylvania, or Blue Shield.

For instance, analysis of a single year of Blue Shield reports picked at random showed that more than 4,681 Blue Shield subscribers underwent surgery to rectify herniated disks, to say nothing of the operations performed on nonmembers. At a conservative estimate, no less than 312,000 people are sweating it out with damaged disks each year, just in the United States.

In another typical year, the Veterans Administration counted a whopping 10,172 aching backs among its applicants for medical care, and of these 5,082, or nearly half, were diagnosed as being caused by defective disks. Those impersonal figures represent a truly forbidding mountain of pain, even though they take into account only those back cases reaching the agency.

That *Journal of Bone and Joint Surgery* mentioned earlier, however, presents an even grimmer aspect. Only a bare 60 per cent of the patients operated on for disk involvment, the *Journal* reports, have been coming away with what could be classified as "long-term results which are satisfactory." They wound up somewhat better off, at least for the time being, but to do it, they had to spend anywhere from fifteen days to two months in the hospital, depending on the type of surgery they got.

By way of contrast, there are also some case records available based on the growing number of patients treated for herniated disks by the use of sclerotherapy.

Solely on the record, 95 per cent of these drew "long-term results which are satisfactory"—meaning cured.

12. THE CURE IN CURARE

BESIDES manipulation and joint sclerotherapy, the other big gun in the war on backache is curare. With these three, most of the back ailments likely to afflict you can be handled.

When it comes to curare, for once the Greeks are out. The ancient Greek fathers of medicine, and a good many of their professional heirs currently in practice, never even heard of it.

The story of the development of this relatively new miracle drug is one of the more colorful dramas in pharmaceutical annals, while the drug itself can rightly be ranked with even the greatest of the so-called wonder drugs. Here is a gripping scenario of scientific discovery amid the retorts, test tubes and the weird apparatus of modern research laboratories, of Spanish treasure ships and Elizabethan adventurers, all seen against the backdrop of mysterious South American jungles. It's the story of a magnificent remedy for pain among civilized men, first brewed in the stewpots of primitive savages.

In one form or another, curare has been around for a long while indeed, historically something like 360 years.

Back in 1844, along about the time in which medical science was beginning to lengthen her skirts and act like a big girl, Dr. Claude Bernard was holding down a brand new chair of physiology at the Sorbonne in Paris.

Before taking up medicine, he'd been pretty good at playwriting, good enough anyhow to write a hit vaudeville comedy called *La Rose du Rhône*. But when Bernard came up with a five-act drama he called *Arthur de Bretagne*, a bilious French critic named Saint-Marc Girardin gave the young author a very fine bit of advice.

"Why don't you try doctoring for a living?" he snarled.

Bernard did exactly that, in fact so well that he is still remembered as the chief pioneer of experimental medicine as well as the architect of modern physiology. Along the line, Dr. Bernard spotted curare's unique affinity for the myoneural junction, thereby opening the door to curare as a useful drug.

As early as 1867, a couple of French doctors, Jousset and

Demine, along with a German named Busch, were already using curare in epilepsy, rabies, chorea (otherwise St. Vitus' Dance), and various muscular tics, but the drug had a long way to go to become the clinically safe and therapeutically certain weapon against pain it is now.

As used in modern medical practice, curare, a rank poison in the raw state, is beyond any doubt a truly outstanding specific for muscle spasm, which amounts to saying that curare represents a virtually immediate cure for the backache you're most likely to get, the simple, uncomplicated symptom found in the overwhelming majority of back-strain cases.

These plain, ordinary, aching backs, the result of over-strain in lifting, of sharp wrenches, twists, sudden bends, and awkward stretches, are the ones most people wind up with. In themselves, they are not particularly dangerous, but like so many other neglected trifles, they may mark the beginning of serious trouble unless properly treated—just as the neglected abrasion can open the door to a fatal case of tetanus.

The accidental bump a man may get while at work in his plant or factory, the glancing blow from a clumsily handled ladder, any and all of the so-called "industrial" accidents can do it. As often as not, a man shrugs such an accident off. He'll maybe allow that it "knocked the wind out of me a little," a fellow worker will rub the spot a bit, and the victim, much embarrassed and anxious to forget the whole thing, goes on with the job as soon as possible. He may have to ignore a little backache and hope it will "wear off" enough for him to come to work the next day. Possibly, it will do just that, but just as possibly it won't.

Or the accident could be an obviously serious one, bad enough to require on-the-spot treatment in the plant infirmary or even hospitalization.

In either case, it's time for curare.

Reporting in the *Journal of the American Medical Asso-*

ciation in 1950, Dr. John D. Fuller presents a whole sheaf of cases he treated with curare in which spasm-induced backache from strains as well as direct injury disappeared in minutes, in some cases after the more familiar narcotic painkillers were tried without success.

WRONG WAY

Among the more serious cases, Dr. Fuller cites the following:

E. S., [Dr. Fuller writes] a man aged twenty-two, was brought to Emergency Hospital, September 23, 1949, after a steel ramp had fallen on his back and knocked him to the ground. He had severe spasms of the upper abdominal muscles and lower anterior chest muscles due to the forcible doubling of his body.

He had severe pain on motion, coughing, and deep breathing. Other than contusions, there was no injury to the abdomen or chest. However, there was a fracture of the upper cervical portion of the spine. His pain was so intense as to make it impossible for him to remain quiet.

RIGHT WAY

Forty minutes after this patient got a shot of curare, he had remarkable freedom from all pain. He slept comfortably that night, and was still feeling good the next day. Another injection was given, with the result that all pain vanished completely. As a result the only treatment needed for the fractured vertebra was bed rest.

At no time was a narcotic or other sedative given or required.

There's Mrs. Y. S., for instance, a routine case from the files of Dr. Shuman. Thirty-nine years old and considerably overweight, Mrs. S. leaned over the edge of a bathtub to lift her youngest son out, and did it all wrong. Instead of stooping with flexed knees beside the tub, so that her powerful leg muscles could have shared the load, Mrs. S. bent directly from the hips, and swung erect with the added weight of the boy thrown directly on to the muscles of her back alone. The result was an immediate, disabling pain—a typical case of strain.

The pain drove her to bed at once. That's where the doctor found her when he arrived at her home the next day, toting his little black bag. She'd had an entirely miserable night. Even now, twenty-four hours after the trouble began, she couldn't as much as roll over in the bed. As long as she could lie still with her electric hot pad turned on to the top notch, it was just bearable. But no more than that.

The spasm was acute, and immediate relief from pain the only object on anybody's mind.

Tucked away in a corner of his bag the doctor had a tiny vial labeled Tubadil. It contained a whitish, syrupy fluid, described on the label as twenty-five milligrams of "d-tubo-curarine per cc." in a "repository menstruum." The stuff, the label read further, was "for intramuscular use only."

The label didn't have to say what the doctor already knew, that if there ever was one, this was a magic painkiller.

Mrs. S. got a l-cc. injection right away. In exactly forty-five minutes the pain slacked off. In an hour, Mrs. S. could move around. She was out of bed five hours later. The next day she was in good enough shape to take manipulative treatments; and a second injection of the doctor's bottled magic, given the third day, left her completely cured. No "side effects," no adverse reactions, and no recurrence of the pains. If Mrs. S. remembers the suffering a bit of careless lifting cost her enough to avoid it, there'll be no more muscle spasm of that kind to need fixing.

What then is curare and how does it work? For one thing, therapeutic curare is not a narcotic, which right away gives it an advantage over habit-forming opiates. Where the narcotics merely blot out perception of the pain, and that for a limited time only, curare on the other hand not only removes the cause of the pain, but furthermore permits almost immediate resumption of muscle function.

It does its work at the critical point of junction between nerve and muscle, called the myoneural junction. There are billions of these neurological command posts in the human body. In effect, these junctions trigger off every muscular motion possible, including those odd twitches everybody gets once in a while, which, incidentally, are nothing to worry about.

It is in the myoneural junctions that every impulse to act, to relax or contract each particular muscle as may be necessary, reaches the muscle from headquarters in the brain or spinal column. Whether the impulse is willed and voluntary, like swinging a golf club, or the uncontrolled, involuntary, and spasmodic contraction of a muscle caused by an injury, those myoneural junctions do the job.

Curare affects these all-important impulse-transmission points in exactly the same way that the more familiar digitalis affects heart muscles. That is to say, that where digitalis affects the heart, and the heart only, so curare affects only the myoneural junctions, blocking them out for a longer or shorter time as desired.

For the patient with the kind of agony set up by a twisting wrench of the spine caused by the wrong kind of lifting, hoisting, or straining of any kind, curare is a true godsend. In genuine muscle spasm, it never fails. It may, perhaps, leave a patient slightly goggle-eyed for a time, which doesn't matter a whoop to the man whose back hurts. What does matter is that curare can bring an immediate, usually permanent end to his suffering.

And best of all, the attending physician needn't be a fancy

consulting specialist. With nothing more than his needle and some know-how, your family doctor can perform this minor miracle right in the patient's bedroom or in his own office.

No sweat.

If curare never did another thing, the way it knocks out torticollis ought to earn it the undying gratitude of long-suffering humanity. Torticollis is doctorese for stiff neck. It is an awkward, uncomfortable inconvenience nobody wants, and anybody stuck with one is understandably anxious to get rid of it quick.

Here also, curare gets rid of the pain by clearing it up, or more accurately, blotting it out at its point of origin, the myoneural junctions involved. It promptly induces a relaxation obtainable otherwise only by deep anesthesia for the tense, spastic muscles setting up the pain.

Curare knocks it out cold. One punch.

13. THE RIDDLE OF CURARE

To the civilized world, curare first emerged from the jungles of South America as a scientific riddle.

For fully four hundred years, curare was to remain a fascinating enigma, challenging the best minds of both Europe and America. Scarcely any drug in modern use has been under scientific investigation longer.

To begin with, curare was simply a curious and highly effective poison used by savages to tip the head of their hunting arrows. The white invaders of the New World knew nothing more about it. Only the Indians knew how to make it, or what jungle plant was the source. Nobody at all knew exactly how it worked. There was no known antidote.

As with many another modern lifesaver and painkiller, curare was originally merely a juice extracted from certain wild plants. In this respect, it shares its ancestry with such medicinal giants as penicillin, reserpine, quinine, cocaine, atropine, and "the one indispensable drug," morphine. Technically, all are classified as alkaloids.

Like a beautiful statue hidden within some shapeless, ugly lump of stone, the true blessings of curare lay concealed in a tarry blob of crudely prepared plant extract, bubbling away in a primitive clay pot.

It quickly gained formal scientific recognition, at least in what passed for scientific thinking in the sixteenth century. A Spanish physician named Nicolas Monardes, who also discovered the principle of fluorescence, made the earliest known attempt to describe the drug, along with its supposed antidotes.

His book, a materia medica of the recently discovered Americas, appeared in an English translation called *Joyfull Newes Out of the Newe Founde Worlde*, published in 1577.

For more than seventy years, Spanish, Italian, and Portugese explorers and adventurers to South America had been bringing back all sorts of fantastic stories about the Americas, and most of them told what they'd learned about curare—which wasn't much.

For instance, there was Bartolomé de Las Casas, whose uncle and father had sailed with Columbus. Bartolomé made a voyage of his own in 1501. He related how the natives, using young girls as decoys, got aboard a ship commanded by Amerigo Vespucci and then showered the crew with poisoned darts. Bartolomé recommended sea water as a cure.

Later, Sir Walter Raleigh described how the Spaniards were torturing the natives to make them reveal the secret process used in the production of crude, raw curare.

In the years that followed, the search for an answer to the riddle of curare went on, pushed by scientific explorers like the great Alexander von Humboldt, outstanding researchers like Dr. C. F. von Martius of Germany, and the Schomburgk brothers, Robert and Richard, whose combined botanical investigations comprised the most important contributions toward solution of the riddle of their times.

Through it all, the solution faced enormous difficulties. Supplies for study were scarce. Samples varied widely, depending chiefly on the production methods used by various tribes. Cooked by traditional, secret formulas steeped in magic, some specimens contained as many as thirty ingredients, others only a few. But gradually, one important facet of the answer began to appear. The key to the effectiveness of curare lay in its relaxing qualities. Introduced into the blood stream, curare would relax muscles in a way no other drug could match. Here was something physicians could use —a muscle-relaxant.

Even while the Schomburgks were clearing up the botanical mysteries surrounding curare, Claude Bernard (1813-1878), the famous French physician we've mentioned before, tore the veil from another face of the enigma. He discovered exactly how the drug works. In addition, Bernard founded modern endocrinology. Both discoveries emerged from his laboratories and both are blazing new paths today.

After Bernard, one break-through followed another. The riddle was crumbling. In 1895 the German chemist Boehm pinned down the essence, fixed and certain, of raw curare. He named his discovery tubocurarine after the bamboo tubes in which his experimental material was originally packed.

In 1935, H. J. King came through with the chemical formula. King published his major analysis in the authoritative *Journal of the Chemical Society* on experiments performed at the National Institute for Medical Research at Hampstead, England. Thereafter, the savages' curare and Boehm's tubocurarine had a new name, d-tubocurarine, and the scientific world had a firm grip on the riddle. As d-tubocurarine, the drug was now perfectly predictable, uniform, and ready for the final experiments and improvements needed to render it entirely safe. That relaxing effect they'd been hunting was already clearly established.

But first there was a supply problem to be licked. King had to work with small quantities of raw curare, mostly museum specimens, and so the quantity of d-tubocurarine produced was strictly limited, just as the first penicillins were scarce, expensive laboratory curiosities until the development of mass-production methods.

It remained for an American explorer, trader, and naturalist, the late Richard C. Gill, to make the next important move in the long, historic march of curare into the ranks of modern medicine. Basically, Gill did two things. First, he identified the Chondrodendron tomentosum, a menispermaceous South American plant, as the exclusive source of Boehm's tubocurarine, and therefore of King's d-tubocurarine. Second, applying American commercial and industrial know-how, Gill established regular supply lines to bring tomentosum in large quantities to his processing plant in Palo Alto, California.

Soon d-tubocurarine was flowing freely into American pharmaceutical houses, to be packaged in aqueous solutions for clinical use by physicians. They put it to work quickly, as a means of inducing relaxation in patients under operative anesthesia. Working in the Homeopathic Hospital of Montreal, Dr. H. R. Griffith as early as 1941 reported excellent results, completely without harmful after effects. In following years, Griffith reported using curare in over three hundred operations on patients of all ages, many classified as poor operative risks. All turned out well, and its use for this purpose is now common.

Others reported successful use in the control of the painful convulsions of tetanus. Dr. A. E. Bennett, of the University of Nebraska College of Medicine, was already using curare to combat the dangerous spasms and violent, bone-breaking contortions appearing in patients receiving shock therapy. This is now standard procedure.

Even so, the aqueous solution by no means exhausted the possibilities opened up by the clinching experiments of Boehm and King. True enough, in anesthesia and shock therapy alone the importance of curare, and its value in operating rooms equipped to handle it safely, was well established almost at once. But doctors like Griffith complained of its fleeting effect in the treatment of such devastating diseases as cerebral palsy, multiple sclerosis, and the crippling after effects of polio, for instance. For these, said Dr. Bennett, ". . . a slow-acting, sustained effect is necessary if the drug is to become a useful therapeutic aid."

By 1950, what the doctors were ordering was on tap.

They specifically wanted a long-acting effect, but one which would begin to work reasonably fast. It wouldn't matter if it turned out to be somewhat slower at going to work than the aqueous solution already in use. And above all, they demanded complete safety—safety to the limit of human fallibility. The antidotes, an absolute antidote called Tensilon and a partial antidote called Prostigmine, were long since available, but now medical men were after a curare they could use anywhere and at any time for a whole series of ailments, including acute backache as well as spastic paraplegia and comparable chronic problems met in daily office practice.

They got it from the research of a brilliant American chemist, Dr. Samuel M. Gordon. A graduate of Tufts in 1922, Dr. Gordon obtained his Ph. D. as a Wrigley Fellow at the University of Wisconsin in 1926, after preliminary work at Iowa in 1923. A fellow of the New York Academy and again a National Research Fellow at Wisconsin, 1926–28, Dr. Gordon took on the job while serving as director of research and vice-president of the Endo Laboratories on Long Island.

Urged by Gill, Gordon based his work on earlier research done at the world famous Mayo Clinic. Gordon found more help in the work previously done by Dr. Jules Freund, then a member of the Research Institute of the City of New York. He also studied the work of Dr. Mary Loveless, of Cornell University Medical School.

The advent of penicillin shed further light on the task in hand, because to some extent the earlier forms of penicillin presented the same problems doctors were meeting in the use of aqueous curare. For both penicillin and curare, the search centered on the development of an ideal menstruum, a physicians' term for some harmless solvent to carry the active drug for safe, prolonged release in the body.

For curare, Dr. Gordon found his ideal menstruum in simple, harmless peanut oil, plus smaller amounts of pure, refined beeswax and a chemical called oxycholesterol, a derivative of the oily secretion found in sheeps' wool.

That did it.

Unlike the aqueous solution, Gordon's new type of curare could be given without the slightest risk of respiratory complications. Aware of this potential danger, the quick-acting earlier types could be used by physicians only where the necessary operating-room equipment to protect the patient was available. They were effective enough, but the swift, full impact of the aqueous solution called for the most careful precautions. But in Gordon's development the desired effect was slowed down and spread out over a relatively long period of time, proceeding at a steady, restrained rate.

Modern curare can be administered with considerably more safety than a shot of penicillin.

As a matter of fact, Dr. Hinton D. Jonez, medical director of St. Joseph Hospital's Multiple Sclerosis Clinic in Tacoma, Washington, has ordered more than one million doses in a six-year period. Furthermore, Dr. Jonez' multiple sclerosis patients themselves have been making their own injections as prescribed, in the same way as thousands of diabetes victims inject themselves with insulin.

As he later reported in the *Journal of the American Medical Association*, Dr. John D. Fuller of Santa Cruz, California, used the new curare in case after case of back injury with equal success and safety.

Dr. Shuman's experience, covering more than five hundred cases of low-back pain with acute spasm and traceable to accidents of one sort or another, has been of exactly the same order.

Comparable reports have been formally presented by men like Dr. Eugene G. Lipow of George Washington University Hospital; Dr. William W. Hoback of Newell Hospital, Chattanooga, Tennessee; Dr. George J. Boines of Wilmington General Hospital, Wilmington, Delaware; Dr. Norris E. Lenahan of St. Anthony Hospital, Columbus, Ohio, and Ohio State University; and Commander John S. Thiemeyer, Jr. of the Medical Corps of the United States Navy.

With all the research, experimentation, testing, and scientific scrutiny applied to curare from earliest times on, it was only natural that the drug would eventually find its place

in the *United States Pharmacopeia*—the national social register of the world's useful drugs.

But not right away, because for a starter curare was accepted into the American Medical Association's super-select list of acceptable drugs, published annually under the title *New and Nonofficial Remedies*.

Screened by a special Council on Pharmacy and Chemistry, no doubtful or outright dangerous drug can possibly win approval. In the words of the Council, "Articles which have only experimental usefulness or whose use involves dangers and disadvantages outweighing their therapeutic value are considered ineligible for inclusion in *New and Nonofficial Remedies."*

The rules carefully set forth every last detail and stipulation to be met, right on down to the name on the label. Permissible advertising is specified; full evidence supporting claims must be given, along with dosages and exact formulas.

While the Council operates on a strictly voluntary basis without official standing, it nevertheless works closely with all the government agencies directly concerned.

There's the Food and Drug Administration to begin with, the federal policing agency; the Federal Trade Commission, with control under the Wheeler-Lea Act of all drug advertising; and the United States Public Health Service, the licensing agency governing all drug products and the production plants making them. The Treasury Department moves in under the Harrison Narcotic Act, and the Post Office Department takes a hand under its powers to prevent fraudulent use of the mails.

To merit a place in *New and Nonofficial Remedies,* curare had to pass muster with all of these as well as the council.

To win a listing in the *Pharmacopeia,* the requirements are even tougher, all things considered. Every five years, this pharmaceutical blue book is completely revised. Obsolete preparations are discarded and newly developed remedies good enough to pass the rigid requirements are admitted.

The national medical, pharmaceutical, and dental associations, The American Chemical Society, drug manufacturers and dealers associations, hospital, food and drug, and public health officials, top medical men from the armed forces, the Surgeon General's office and the National Bureau of Standards set up what is in effect a blue-ribbon jury to guarantee as far as humanly possible the purity, effectiveness, and above all the safety of any drug meriting this seal of approval.

Modern curare made it in 1950.

It is only a question of time before curare will be produced synthetically and our present dependence on South American sources eliminated. The experiments are already under way.

The dedicated work of thousands—scientists, physicians, naturalists, obscure toilers in hundreds of laboratories over hundreds of years—have gone into the forging of this mighty weapon in man's conquest of pain.

But the final honor must go to Dr. Gordon.

In his perfection of a simple and safe curare, available to any physician for office use, Dr. Gordon flung open the last door leading to the practical, everyday use of curare.

The riddle was solved.

14. SOME CURES, SOME SCIENTIFIC

THE SWIFTLY expanding field of endocrinology is already firmly established as a potential area for inconceivable progress in the relief of human distress of all kinds. It is not surprising, then, to find this newest of the healing arts playing an increasingly important part in the treatment of low-back disorders.

Endocrinology begins with an appraisal of the workings of a number of very wonderful and, as yet, only partly understood glands in your body, called the glands of internal secretion. These glands, such as the thyroid, parathyroid, pituitary, pineal, suprarenal, and thymus, are also known as the ductless glands. Located in various parts of the head and body, each produces one or more very important secretions, which are discharged directly into the blood stream.

Fortunately, medical research has learned how to duplicate nearly all of these secretions.

As of now, endocrinology may often be the best answer to some painful forms of spinal arthritis, cancer of the spine, and certain types of relatively infrequent but nonetheless disabling backaches resulting from disorders of the important thyroid glands—small, shield-shaped organs located in the base of the throat on either side of the windpipe.

134

Should diagnosis disclose your backache to be one of the spinal arthritic types, the use of cortisone or one of several substances secreted by the pituitary gland may be effective.

In a typical case, one particular pituitary synthetic, called ACTH, which directly affects the suprarenal, or adrenal glands, may be given. Here's another queer medical word that can't be blamed on the Greeks. Actually, the word is an artificial name derived from the initial letters of the words adreno-cortico-tropic-hormone, meaning a special kind of juice sure to jazz up the cortisone-producing department of the adrenal glands.

This stepped-up cortisone production immediately does a lot of things. For one, it effectively reduces the characteristic inflammation set up by arthritis. For another, it also cools off any other inflammatory condition present, which may or may not be good.

However, as far as medical science can figure, this reduction of arthritic inflammation is a very fine thing indeed, which is just exactly what the patient is also likely to think, because this inflammation is what makes the arthritic joint stiffen up and hurt. As a matter of fact, until we had ACTH-cortisone, the best anybody could recommend for arthritis of the back was good old aspirin, which simply deadened the pain a little.

But that wasn't because no one was trying, because nearly all of the medical profession was banging away at arthritis with a lot of procedures, a good many of which surprisingly enough are still in use. A good many of them, however, are strictly for the birds.

One school of thought, dedicated no doubt to the proposition that gold is pretty good stuff any way you want to take it, holds that arthritic backaches yield to massive injections of nice, raw, shiny, metallic gold dust, put up in what is called a colloidal solution.

The procedure is impressively expensive and, as often as not, may give the patient the itch, or a bellyache, or something called agranulocytosis. Medicine being what it is, some of the arthritics are reported to have decided they felt better. Let's hope they do.

There's another well-established line of thinking, some of which still persists, to the effect that there's nothing wrong with a backache of supposedly arthritic origin that a good, sound, substantial bowel movement can't fix. One is good, more is better, and a lot is best of all. So cathartics are prescribed.

Epsom salts, Glauber's salt, cascara (otherwise the CC tablet of military fame), sulphur in one form or another, phenolphthalein, milk of magnesia, agar, mineral oil, ox bile and the like, not to mention castor oil and a good, honest enema, all get a whirl. If they don't do any good, it is always possible to fall back on a relatively new notion summed up in the term, "focal infection."

This means that an abscessed tooth maybe, or your infected tonsils, a sick gall bladder, or your appendix perhaps, is cooking up poisonous substances that somehow hit you in the elbow, knee, hip, or spine, or any other movable bony structure. Just to get the girls into focus, ovaries too became suspect, and about twenty years ago, any number of practicing physicians were recommending removal of these parts as a cure for arthritis. But the doctors calling for surgical excision of ovaries, gall bladders, teeth, appendixes, or whatever as a backache cure had competition, you may be sure.

Possibly the oddest suggestion came from the therapeutic bee-sting merchants.

Some physicians, all of them holders of duly registered, legal credentials, got it into their heads that arthritis could be fixed up by sicking an infuriated bee, or a hornet, or maybe a wasp, onto the patient. People in the bee business, out

to promote honey or any other profitable pitch, began to give out testimonials about how getting stung by bees cured J. J. Whoever of his arthritis.

Besides the chronic kind, there are about twenty-three other varieties of arthritis in the medical dictionaries, like acute gouty, and acute rheumatic, and atrophic, gonorrheal, deformans neoplastica, dental, hypertrophic, proliferative, suppurative, and such.

But so long as the trouble could be diagnosed as arthritis of any kind, getting stung by a bee ought to fix it up, according to these doctors. Of course, the arthritis in hand might be anything from acute gouty to suppurative, but who'd want to quibble?

While the medical profession of the United States, and the American laity alike were heehawing about how Communist medicos were hanging live leeches on Joe Stalin to slack off his blood pressure, some American doctors were still enlisting the services of live bees in an effort to alleviate arthritis. As carried out in any number of hospital clinics, this bee-sting ritual was a first-class dilly.

On B-day, the arthritic patients would line up in the clinic, and in due time the assisting apiarist, who raised the bees, would arrive with a little box containing a score or so of choice performers.

When everybody and everything was ready, the head doctor would appear and, wielding a pair of shiny tweezers, he would dip into the little box and grab hold of a bee already buzzing mad. Then the doctor would solemnly put the bee on the patient, by pressing the angry insect against the back, or wherever the arthritis was supposed to be.

Then the bee, irritated beyond all measure, would cut loose and shoot the works, after which, having served mankind, the bee would crawl into some corner of the clinic and die, and the delighted patient would go away until the next time. After a while, more advanced physicians began injecting their patients with formic acid, which was all the bees had to offer in the first place. By either method, bees or injection, the results were about the same.

In odd places around the countryside, such methods are still in use, but by and large ACTH and cortisone are now the principal weapons against arthritis. For many reasons, physicians have increasingly elected to prescribe cortisone directly, rather than the ACTH. Either is generally regarded as a vast improvement over such things as gold injections, cathartics, and focal-infection gambits, all of which are still occasionally heard from.

For that matter, anybody really sold on bee-stings may even now find a medical die-hard ready to put the bee on him.

Besides ACTH and cortisone, there's another glandular secretion called thyroxin, produced by the thyroid glands, which carries a lot of weight as far as your health is concerned.

If the trouble is due to too little thyroxin, they call it hypothyroidism. A frequent secondary symptom of this condition is a dull, wearying, and persistent backache—just another example of the countless ways in which you can get into trouble with your back. This type of backache often responds well to doses of thyroid.

All of these hormonal secretions, thyroxin, cortisone, ACTH, and such, are of vast significance to be sure, but none compete therapeutically with one super-special group of hormones. These are the famous sex hormones, about which almost everybody knows something but hardly anybody knows enough.

The use of the sex hormones in numbers of ways for various purposes is a matter of daily medical practice, going far beyond the common notion that the whole use of sex hormones is to make sure that men will have hairy chests and women will be truly double-breasted. Like sex in general, the sex hormones are involved in pretty nearly everything related to your body.

For lack of a sufficient supply of the sex hormone, as with any other hormonal deficiency, your metabolism can be out of balance. You can possibly wind up with osteoporosis and consequent backache. The indicated procedure here, of course, is to give the patient carefully calculated doses of the proper hormones to restore the balance.

Naturally enough, these same sex hormones get a heavy play in the care and treatment of cancer of the prostate, an especially nasty source of backache. Fortunately, it is relatively rare.

In such cases, the hormone treatment generally favored affords a good example of the repressive aspect of hormone therapy. Doses of the female hormone tend to inhibit the normal growth and function of the diseased prostate, including the cancerous tissue involved. At the same time, castration is ordinarily advisable in order to eliminate the natural stimulus of the prostate induced by the testicular secretion of testerone, the male hormone.

Where the cancer has had a chance to spread to surrounding areas to such an extent that surgery is deemed no longer effective, the hormonal treatment becomes just about the last resort possible.

Unquestionably, as to cancer anywhere, the best approach to cancer of the prostate is dependent on early discovery and prompt surgery. However, the fact remains that more progress has been made in the treatment of prostatic cancer than all other manifestations, and the medical casebooks are full of instances in which victims of this erstwhile killer have been granted many, many more years of pain-free life, thanks to hormones.

It goes without saying that they got rid of their backache.

One more variety of backache, in the same general category of those usually associated with the several glandular disorders, is the backache you get when, for any one of a number of reasons, your blood develops excessive amounts of uric acid. A simple laboratory test readily discloses the condition, after which it can be treated by a preparation derived principally from a substance called benzoic acid.

Admittedly, such treatment isn't a definite cure, but the treatment is so convenient—a few tablets taken daily—that most patients with this kind of a backache are satisfied to let well enough alone.

For them, well enough simply means no backache.

15. IT'S ALL IN YOUR HEAD?

YOUR BACKACHE could be psychosomatic.

In other words, backache can be the result not of some injury, structural deficiency, physical disease or the like, but of some mental, emotional, or psychic disturbance. In short, backache can be psychogenic.

Let's suppose for the moment that none of the examinations you may have had has turned up any physical clue as to what's causing your trouble. Everything—spine, pelvis, the body's functional organs right on down to your appendix, if you still have it—checks out just fine. In other words, by ordinary standards you are healthy. Nothing wrong with you.

But there you sit, with a backache hurting like sin. It's a genuine backache. It's not imaginary. You've got the tense muscles, the stiffness, the rigid, awkward body posture and all the soreness anybody with a backache ever had. Why?

It's time to start thinking about inner conflicts.

Almost no one, things being the way they are, is absolutely free of such conflicts. But if the conflicts become literally painful and impose drastic limits on your life, you will want to resolve them as quickly as possible, and for this you may need help from a psychiatric specialist. The advances made in this field in just the last fifty years or so have made it possible to deal with many emotional problems before they get out of hand, and your aching back may be your body's way of letting you know that it's time to start dealing. The dread that once was felt at the possibility of "mental" illness has been dissipated to a large degree by understanding. In some circles, as a matter of fact, a course in psychotherapy is nearly as good as a Thunderbird as an indication of status.

Like many another new therapeutic notion, psychiatry has actually been around a long, long while. Certainly its general principles were under study long before Dr. Sigmund Freud made household words out of such terms as Oedipus complex, inhibitions, frustrations, sublimation, inferiority and

superiority, ego and superego, subconscious, unconscious, suppression and repression, libido and id.

Hippocrates as usual was on the beam. He probably pinned down firmly the earliest taproot of psychiatry by attributing organic disorders, unexplained anxieties, fears, and terrors to mental, that is to say, psychic origins. "All these things," said he, "we endure from the brain." The brain, he explained, might be suffering from some "preternatural or unusual affection."

A good hundred years later, Plato was telling the rest of the Greeks how the Athenian medical men were missing the boat by their neglect of what we now call psychiatry. "For this is the great error of our day . . . " he lamented, "that physicians separate the soul from the body."

Medieval Arabian physicians also got to be pretty smart about psychiatry. The medical chronicles of the times tell, for instance, how a famous Arabian doctor named Rhazes, who died in 923 A.D., cured the King's rheumatism by ordering him into a hot bath. Then, as the unarmed and unattended monarch sat helpless in his birthday suit soaking his stiff, aching joints, Dr. Rhazes whipped out a big knife and threatened to slit his throat. Naturally, the King flipped. In a royal fury, he hopped to his feet as nimble as an acrobat. Roaring for blood, he bellowed for the palace guard, but Rhazes lit out of there on a very fast horse. Obviously that "rheumatism" was all in the King's head. In other words, it was a psychogenic condition, and Dr. Rhazes had done a fine job before he had to run for his life.

But the King hadn't heard the last of his intrepid physician.

A week or so later, Rhazes sent the King a little note. The hot bath treatment he'd been giving him "would have been unduly protracted," he wrote, "so I abandoned it in favor of psychotherapeusis. . . ." He'd deliberately pulled that

knife, he confessed, to jolt the King out of his psychosomatic rheumatism. And the King, like many another patient, had to admit that after all doctor knows best.

In gratitude he forced his daring benefactor to accept a "robe of honor, a cloak, a turban, arms and a male and female slave, and a horse fully caparisoned, and further assigned to him a yearly pension of two thousand gold dinars and two hundred ass-loads of corn." Psychiatric care is still pretty expensive.

Like all medicine, the branch of medicine we now call psychiatry has come a long way towards therapeutic maturity. To be sure, the scientific Donnybrook under way since Freud's time is still disturbing the peace among practicing psychiatrists.

But nobody any longer denies either the scientific validity or therapeutic usefulness of the main body of experience-tested psychiatric practice. Accordingly, if you have a psychosomatic backache, your best bet for getting rid of it is through the professional ministrations of a psychiatrist.

It could happen to you, just as it has happened to others

every bit as sane as you are, and almost any physician you may consult can cite examples.

Take the lady we're going to call Mrs. Jane Smith, which of course isn't her name. Mrs. Smith fought it out with a nagging, miserable backache for years.

A normally cheerful, well-behaved housewife around forty, she was even something of a looker. Through seventeen years of marriage she'd been as happy as the next one, even if Mr. Smith hadn't turned out to be quite the shining dreamboat he looked like on her wedding day.

But beneath the outward façade of a reasonably happy marriage, things were going on way down inside Mrs. Smith through the years, little psychic wounds caused by her disapproval of her husband's behavior. Nothing particularly big, nor anything she could really put her finger on. Of course, like many another wife, Mrs. Smith often felt that her husband wasn't too smart about his business, and didn't manage the family finances very well.

Both were fond of their little daughter, and their common affection helped smooth over the little frictions of daily life. But in Mrs. Smith's innermost being, little frictions were building up year after year, buried away as a mounting, though unconscious complex of resentments and frustrations.

Eventually, it all came to a head.

Her husband's business fell off. Faced with disaster, he worked harder and longer. He was home less, and when he was home there were quarrels, quarrels after which he began to turn more and more to their daughter for solace and affection. In response Mrs. Smith felt neglected, insecure, and unhappy, and physical reactions soon appeared—bad ones.

First off, their formerly well-adjusted sex relationship broke down. Their sex life had already begun to deteriorate, from the standpoint of frequency as well as satisfaction, both because of the husband's preoccupation with his failing business and her hidden emotional conflict. For Mrs. Smith, what had once been romantic fun became an unpleasant duty. Worse yet, she got physically sick following intercourse, which now invariably led to nausea and vomiting.

To top it off, Mrs. Smith finally developed the backache which brought her to the doctor's office.

There was no physical impairment in evidence as a cause. The mere lack of a physical cause for her low-back pain wasn't enough in itself to establish her complaint as a psychosomatic backache, but her otherwise inexplicable reaction to sex was vastly significant. Her sexual problem was the key to the diagnosis.

In psychiatric terminology, it represented a typical exam-ample of "organ language," in other words, the special way in which emotions, feelings, or thoughts can be expressed which cannot be conveyed by either words or actions. Mrs. Smith, through her digestive organs by nausea and vomiting, and through her back by muscle spasm and pain, merely expressed her deep-rooted resentment, anxiety, and emotional disappointment concerning her husband.

This was a typical psychogenic backache. The backache effectively prevented her from performing the body motion essential to the sex act. Thus intimacy with her husband, whom she had come to hate, became impossible.

The vomiting represented a similar symbolic rejection.

Real or fancied neglect by a husband preceded by a child-hood history of actual or imagined neglect at the hands of parents sets the stage many times for psychosomatic illness in later years. What's sauce for the goose is also sound psychiatry for the gander, and the husband can get himself a psycho-somatic illness out of the marriage relationship every bit as easily as the wife can, and for essentially the same causes. He can also get himself a full-fledged, first-class, and hurt-like-the-devil-backache out of his job, without ever lifting anything heavier than his pay check.

Whether he's a bank clerk, or an auto mechanic, a laboratory research man, hardware salesman, advertising executive, truck driver, plumber, or the headwaiter in a night club, a man can fetch up with a genuine backache complete with all the accessories, all the symptoms, and all the pain he needs to put him right out of action.

The man isn't faking. His backache is psychogenic, rooted in the depths of an underlying neurosis, and it's every bit as real as any backache set up by some physical ailment.

To identify his aching back as a psychogenic proposition isn't to declare flatly that it's entirely in his head, or in his inner tensions, frustrations, repressions, or psychological make-up. Like any other psychosomatic ailment, such a back condition most frequently presents some combination of physical and neurotic factors, each of which may figure in the total problem to varying degrees. The backache in question could be largely a physical problem, plus a minor neurotic factor, or it could be primarily neurotic with a lesser physical basis.

For instance, a man might be getting by fairly well with some less serious back disorder, a spinal osteoporosis perhaps. He'd be putting up with mild but chronic pain, some days not so good, some days not so bad, but bearable most of the time. He's an eight-to-five desk hand with some insurance company, possibly, but even when it's bad the back isn't interfering with his work to any extent. He's doing all right. His job is going fine. His wife and home are all a man could desire.

That's the way it was, we'll suppose, until something happened to knock the bottom out of his world—the afternoon he got home unexpectedly early to find his wife on the daven-

148

port with a friend, a golfing companion he'd always regarded as a real pal.

He of course packed up and got out. While awaiting his divorce, he moved into a drab hotel room, dropped all of his friends, and settled down to an empty, embittered existence supported only by the routine of his job.

But the psychic injury, or trauma, delivered by the betrayal and the destruction of his home, in addition to the long-standing physical disorder in his back, added up to an intolerable condition. His back flared up bad enough to cost him the job he could no longer handle. Between the basic physical impairment and the superimposed emotional upset, the back disorder had developed into a crippling handicap.

149

By way of further illustration, the resentments and anxieties accumulated by an auto mechanic from childhood on, exploded at last by irritation engendered by a nagging mother-in-law, found an action outlet in an overwork response. He drove himself far beyond his physical capacity in an unconscious emotional reaction. The end result was a bad case of fibrositis of the back. His disorder was physical in nature, but psychogenic at the bottom.

As a matter of sound psychiatric experience, low-back pain is now well recognized as a common consequence of anxieties, unconscious resentments, and similar emotional disturbances. Such a psychogenic back can well open the door to hasty, mistaken diagnosis, and even an unnecessary operation in some instances.

Of these, one prominent psychiatrist has grimly observed: "I shudder when I think of the laminectomies and fusions done on obviously neurotic people without psychiatric consultation."

Another expressed himself as frankly amazed at the number of patients whose only need was for psychotherapy who got completely useless lumbar punctures, myelograms, laminectomies, and corrective braces. When at long last the psychiatrist is called in, the case is by then hopelessly complicated by operative tissue damage, or even narcotic addiction induced by the long-continued use of opium-based pain pills.

Certainly no type of surgery is going to do a genuinely psychogenic back any good, which amounts to saying that it can only do harm.

On the other hand, if a thorough, complete examination of your back should disclose a few physical defects, there is still no reason to conclude that these in themselves are the sole or even a partial cause of your backache. Many a man has gone along for years without a moment's distress from a slightly herniated disk nobody knew he had, until at last some psychogenic disturbance precipitated a backache. Careful diagnosis then may disclose not only the psychogenic factor, but also the previously unsuspected disk injury.

It is seldom that even the closest observation or the most searching examination can be relied upon to establish a sharp line of demarcation between the physical and psychogenic factors in back cases of this kind, and management of this type of case admittedly presents the greatest difficulty.

In World War II, "Oh, my aching back" soon became the plaint of harassed soldiers in front lines as well as the training camps back home, and the wryly humorous cry of distress didn't come only from Army goldbricks. For many a man struggling with the anxieties, mental stresses, and unavoidable discomforts of war, not to mention the normal fear of ever-present death, the cry too often expressed serious, neurotic indications.

In the Mediterranean Theater alone, an Army survey reported that fully 40 per cent of the musculoskeletal disorders originated mainly in emotional disturbance. The most common psychosomatic symptom listed was low-back pain.

Among civilians the psychogenic back emerging in response to a neurotic, overmastering need for attention and emotional dominance, both within the family and in wider groups, is no rarity. Nor is it uncommon to find a partly or even entirely psychogenic backache originating in a latent fear of the boss, jealousy of business rivals, competitive anxieties, performance inadequacies, and the like.

It must be remembered that such backaches are in no sense simulated, assumed, or "faked." They are real pains, causing real distress, and they are to be removed only by expert care.

To be sure, your neurosis could register physically in many ways, in psychogenic gastric disturbances, for instance, or impotence, frigidity, heart trouble, asthma—anything, in fact, from a mild colitis to complete loss of sight. But psychiatric experience clearly places your back definitely in the picture as a prime target for neurotic tensions underlying physical impairment because your back includes such an important part of the entire nervous system.

The very words and familiar phrases of common speech set the neurasthenic stage. We call it a "back-breaking job," or refer to a hen-pecked husband as "a spineless jerk," and the guy who lets himself be pushed around as having "no backbone." Similarly the back-slapping, glad-hander who thinks he's the life of the party, in the minds of others is just another "pain in the neck."

To the trained psychiatrist, the patient who limps in with his back bent, twisted, and wracked with psychogenic pain, the posture alone speaks at least as loud as, and sometimes louder than, words. No matter what the psychiatric patient wants to say about his aching back, to the searching eye and discerning mind of his physician, the back itself is putting up the real story, the unvarnished truth of the matter about which the patient consciously knows nothing at all.

In that "organ language" which only the back and the doctor understand, the afflicted patient is saying things like, "My cross is too heavy to bear—this load is breaking my back—I've got to have help—I can't work any more—don't compel me to have sex—love me and care for me the way my mother did."

Among women, the appearance of a psychogenic low-back pain is frequently encountered in connection with some slight and unimportant inward defect of the sex organs. Too insignificant to be harmful, it could be ignored except for a firmly fixed though mistaken notion of both the patient and the doctor that this condition is causing the backache.

But the low-back pain, psychogenic and in no wise related to the minor organic disorder to begin with, hangs on even after surgery has cleared up the supposed cause. Such cases measure the extent to which many patients, and more than a few doctors as well, would rather resort to surgery than accept a neurosis as the real source of a low-back symptom.

And finally, there is still another aspect of the psychogenic backache that must be born in mind. The doctor in charge could be entirely wrong.

Unable to find anything else the matter with you and unwilling to give up, he just might find it easier to label your problem as a job for psychiatry, and either turn you over to a specialist in such problems or start digging into your neurasthenic Shangri-La on his own.

If he does, anything might happen. You might even get well.

As we said at the beginning of this chapter, your aching back could be a psychosomatic proposition, either altogether or to a greater or less degree. If your backache turns out to be primarily psychogenic, you'll do well to put yourself into the hands of the best psychiatric physician you can induce to take your case.

But along about now a small word of caution may be in order.

For heaven's sake don't start reading up on a lot of books about psychiatry from the corner news-stand with some idea of resolving your own inner conflicts. The less you yourself know about psychiatric techniques, the easier it will be for a professional psychiatrist to get you untangled mentally and spiritually, and therefore the sooner your psychogenic backache will vanish. Your psychiatrist is above all a physician who is a specialist in dealing with those delicately balanced, enormously important and critical forces lying deep in the innermost core of your being. The hordes of amateur drawing-room psychiatrists cluttering up the landscape are not only asinine, but potentially dangerous meddlers. Only an

egotistical fool will presume to rush into the sacred, private temple of your God-given personality.

Psychiatry, says the medical dictionary, is "that branch of medicine which deals with the disorders of the psyche." And the psyche, it further explains, is "The mind; the mental life including both conscious and unconscious processes."

It's Greek again, taken from a mythological dish named Psyche who figured as Cupid's best girl. According to the Greeks, this beautiful maiden also represented the human soul, or mind, which is what your psychiatrist will be working on to cure your psychosomatic back, if that's what you have.

But in any case, the probability that you've got a psychosomatic back is slim enough for comfort, assuming you'd rather have a slipped disk, for instance, than a neurosis.

Physical impairment of some kind is at the bottom of a good 90 per cent of the backache problem.

So let's not get neurotic about it.

16. HEAVEN HELPS HIM . . .

THE VAST BULK of all backache is avoidable. In the main, there are only three simple considerations you need be careful about. These are first of all, how you handle yourself when making any extra, unusual physical effort, particularly lifting, and what kind of clothing you wear, and what you eat.

Except for a few conditions like osteitis condensans, cancer, and uncontrollable developmental defects, along with accidental injuries suffered in falls, automobile collisions, and similar mishaps, all of the backache limping around could probably have been avoided by the observance of a few easily understood and not inconvenient precautions.

Within this area, improper lifting of heavy objects is the hands-down source of most of the trouble. A lot more is traceable to general pushing, hauling, reaching, twisting, and physical overexertion of all kinds.

To go back to those Greeks again, it turns out that Archimedes, a mathematician who spent some time as an Athenian combat engineer, doped out a few fresh ideas on levers, pinch bars, weight-lifting and such, which, as any doctor knows and you ought to know, are of terrific importance to your back. Archimedes came up with facts and figures to show scientifically why you can't lift a bucket of water under certain conditions. Anybody's welcome to try.

Just put a bucket of water on the kitchen table. Stand at arm's length and firmly grasp the handle of the bucket. Now heave straight up. No elbow bending of any kind, and no bending at the waist. The man, woman, or child who can as much as get that bucket half an inch off the table is very tough indeed. Anybody who can hold it there for a whole minute can get a job with the circus side show anytime.

Now put the bucket on the floor. Step in close, with one foot at either side, and using knee, hip, and back joints, lower your upper body downward and grasp the handle. It's about the way a modest dame stoops to pick up her marbles, supposing she wants the marble game to continue.

156

In this position, anybody in the room, including kids barely tall enough to top the bucket, can easily heave it up. What's more, the bucket can be held as long as anybody's fool enough.

Without bothering about all the Greek science, the general idea ought now to be clear enough, and the idea applies to any kind of lifting, hauling, or shoving you do. A person who constantly keeps this simple notion in mind stands at least a 50 per cent better chance of escaping all kinds of painful, expensive back injuries, including one of the commonest of avoidable conditions, a damaged vertebral disk.

The good chances are that right now, this minute, you are wearing a cotton undershirt. If, as a matter of fact, you're reading in bed and actually wearing pajamas, then the undershirt you were wearing is in the laundry hamper. That shirt has a good deal to do with your back. Here's why.

Next to foolish lifting, the most prolific source of back disorders in general is nothing more or less than plain, ordinary, and entirely avoidable chilling. From the standpoint of what it can do to your back, a sudden chill is a serious matter, too often ignored as a trifling discomfort, and seldom recognized for the menace it actually represents. It can happen to anybody, depending largely on the aforesaid shirt.

Consider Joe Doakes on a spring evening.

Joe has a little home in the suburbs. Professionally, he's an invoice clerk for a mail-order house. But right now a seed catalogue has him all excited about his lawn.

This day in early April finds him gulping down a hasty meal, vetoing a demand that he take his wife and children to the movies, and heading outdoors with a spading fork.

An hour later he has a patch of ground spaded and ready for seed, and he's dripping with perspiration—what he calls a "good healthy sweat." He stops to chat with a neighbor and lets his shirt dry on his back. He's setting the stage for a possible nasty disk involvement a few years later.

Sooner than that—a day or a week later—he has the first result, a painful backache brought on by sweat and strain. It's a pity because, with only the simplest of precautions, the trouble could have been avoided—something as simple as slipping on a sweatshirt or a jacket after finishing the job.

Most of the undergarments on the haberdashery shelves these days are straight cotton, and undershirts containing even a little wool are admittedly a bit more expensive, but as a protection against backache due to sudden chill, such wool-cotton, or even all-wool, shirts are cheap at twice the price. Doctors' fees are high, and getting higher.

Fashions being what they are, protective underwear for

women is admittedly a problem. But any girl who can afford to sacrifice romance for utility presumably could wear cotton-wool longies with profit, if only for strenuous outdoor activity. She can certainly slip on a sweater or warm jacket after heavy exercise.

And she can also wear sensible, low-heeled shoes as often as the occasion will allow. There's no good reason why a housewife should mince around on spikes while dusting the living room.

Getting back to Joe, he could have done two more simple things to avoid that strain. He might have elected to do a little study on the art and science of swinging a shovel, in which case that business with a bucket of water would point to the right basic principle. And taking into account the obvious differences between his regular routine and his agricultural pursuits, he might have made a two-day job of the spading instead of knocking off the whole operation in one session—just a matter of taking it easy.

All of which is by way of offering a very fine piece of medical advice at no extra charge.

Don't be a Joe!

With the best intentions in the world, this story can no longer sidestep a bad word.

It's time to talk about d-i-e-t.

But the diet talk coming up here has nothing to do with the usual stuff about getting fat people skinny or skinny people fat. Aside from anything else, what you eat can become directly responsible for two pain-producing bone diseases due to a lack of vitamins in your food.

One, called rickets, is basically a childhood complaint while the other, named osteomalacia, is an adult disease. Both are generically related.

Rickets as a word is another one that can't be charged off to the ancient Greeks. The word is derived directly from the ultimate effect the disease causes in those who come down with it. They get rickety. The legs, arms, and bony structure in general become tottery and shaky.

Rickets is about the most easily avoided disease in the whole range of childhood complaints. If there isn't enough income to provide such vitamin-D rich foods as cod-liver oil, eggs, fish, or butter, there's no charge for letting a child soak up sunshine, the greatest vitamin source of all. Rickets is inexcusable.

In its adult form it's called osteomalacia, and its prevention calls for the same measures: large helpings of vitamin D in the diet and lots of sunshine.

But no matter what, things do happen, and you may some-day be in trouble with a bad backache despite all precautions.

The brainiest, most intelligent, effective, well-advised, sound, solid, and sensible thing you can do is call your doctor right away. If you don't have one, get one, but by all means call one.

Go to bed. Of all things you can do to help, this is beyond all question the most important. If you can take it for a few minutes, you can't go wrong with a hot tub bath or shower first, followed by a brisk toweling. But hurry to bed. It will do you more good than all the salves, liniments, plasters, rubbing solutions, or whatever you may have in the medicine chest or on tap at the corner drug store. You can apply a heating pad if you think you have to, but don't be disappointed if nothing happens.

Get flat on your back.

There's just a chance that tucking a tightly rolled Turkish towel under the small of your back may help. And you may get a little relief out of lying first on one side and then on the other. If you must get up, get it over with quick.

Don't protract the agony of pushing up out of a bed or off a chair with your arms in an effort to take it easy. Here, the pitch is the same as the "quick-rip" method for removing adhesive plaster. If you are coming up off a chair, set your feet, take a couple of trial swings from the hip and get it over with. One quick upward lurch, and you're on your feet. If in bed, lie on your side facing out and let your legs, knees together, drop down. Use this leverage to swing your upper body vertical.

It may help a little, too, if you'll just remember that back-ache never killed anybody, even though you may find yourself wishing it could before you're through.

As soon as the doctor can get to you, he should have you feeling better in a few minutes—at least temporarily. He

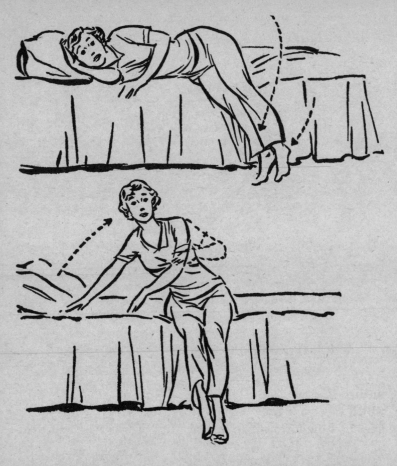

may even tell you exactly what's wrong right off the bat, in which case pay him his fee as quickly as possible and call up a good doctor.

Assuming you have a good one to begin with, the thing to do next is to agree on a course of treatment, based naturally, on the best preliminary diagnosis the doctor can make. This is admittedly only a tentative diagnosis, but it must be made because getting you fixed up has to start somewhere.

162

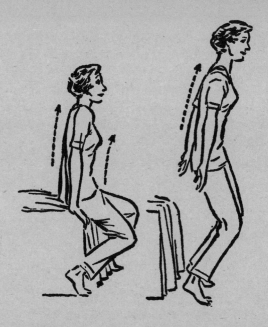

However, if you don't start going places within a reasonable number of office visits, or in about three or four weeks,
it's time to resurvey. You could be in the clutches of a
medico dedicated to some pet treatment or another, in
which case your only chance of getting better is for you to
have had the foresight to get the kind of backache this treatment cures.

In short, unless you're entirely satisfied with what's going
on, the admission price entitles you to do a certain amount
of judicious "needling." You may very properly ask what
goes, and you don't have to settle for some soothing murmurs
as an answer.

It's always in order, and can't possibly give offence, to ask
your doctor if he'd like a little consultation, for instance.

There's just one more thing—don't worry.

The natural ability of your body to endure shock, to restore itself, and weather storms, the tremendous reserves of vitality and the vast recuperative powers we all have, can produce amazing results even without help—and sometimes in spite of it.

"Don't worry" has been good medical advice ever since Hippocrates was telling people, "Life is short, and the Art long; the occasion fleeting; experience fallacious; and judgment difficult."

So why worry?

17. DO IT YOURSELF

IT'S YOUR back. Whether it's healthy or ailing, you're the only person alive who can do anything about it.

The best doctors in the world, the latest discoveries of science, the last word in medical art can do no more than help you to help nature in the job of keeping well to begin with, and getting well again if you don't.

And so it's up to you to do something, not only in connection with that back of yours, but for your whole mental and physical make-up. Here the main role you can play in your own salvation can be defined in just two words—exercise and diet.

There's no question but that walking—simple pick-'em-up and lay-'em-down walking—is the greatest exercise ever developed.

What's more, it's good for you, no matter what, and even if your aching back is aching like to kill you, you ought to walk as much as you can stand.

To be sure, this kind of therapeutic heresy isn't at all popular with those schools of medical nonsense hung up on getting everybody to bed as soon as possible for as long as possible, this being usually the length of time the patient's medical insurance has to run.

In fact, the medical journals get a nice bit of revenue out of ads for various painkillers—professionally the word is "muscle relaxants"—which repeat in print what many a back patient is told in private. "There is no alternative or substitute for bed rest," they proclaim, along with a picture of a nice, deep mattress bed.

This fine, ringing declaration sounds convincing enough, but as helpful advice in the treatment of backache of any kind, this assertion is simply a whole lot of nothing, totally wrong and entirely untrue.

The fact of the matter is that such immobilization, such complete restriction of motion, such deliberate lack of activity is just one thing—harmful.

Actually and understandably, it is quite possible for your back to be aching so badly that real honest-to-goodness walking is out of the question: that you simply can't manage it because of the pain.

But even here, you ought to be able to get in some motion, some bit of movement, some body activity; and the more of it you can manage, the sooner you'll be entirely well. This may mean as little as rolling over to lie face down, for a starter. Bit by bit, you may work up to a hands and knees position, and this is all to the good.

Patients attempting this often find that the increased agony they feared simply never happens. Given a good doctor's reassurance, they find themselves able to make, literally, a lot of moves toward getting well, a little at a time.

The most likely one is a simple backward-forward rocking motion while on the hands and knees. With a little determination, you may even get to sit up a bit. After all, if you get too tired, or start to hurt too much, you can always lie down again, which is where you started.

But the try will put you ahead of the game, even if you may not get any farther than rolling over the first time around, because of the exercise involved. You've stimulated your circulation, however slightly, and you've done a little bit, again however slight, toward breaking up that pain-spasm-pain cycle mentioned earlier in this book, and you'll find yourself in a better frame of mind about the whole thing as soon as you realize, as a result, that you are neither entirely helpless nor ready for permanent consignment to the scrap yard.

With a little more effort, which admittedly may be a bit painful but not hopelessly painful, you may be able to be up and around on crutches. When that happens, you've just about got it licked.

You'll be able to come to the table for meals, instead of eating off a teetering bed tray. You'll be using the bathroom instead of that lousy bedpan, and you won't any longer have to depend on having somebody around all the time to bring you every little thing you need.

It is only now, in this final half of the twentieth century, that the medical profession is beginning to understand the overriding importance of avoiding the atrophy and self-accelerating decline induced by long periods of confinement in bed.

Modern medicine now recognizes the value of getting the patient into active movement again as soon as at all possible, and it is not at all unusual for operative patients to walk straight from the operating room back to their beds. It's called early ambulation.

Says Dr. Sedgwick Meade, writing in the *Journal of the American Medical Association* in 1962, "As were the fads of bleeding and calomel purging, which preceded it, the vogue of rest has been grossly overused, and it has persisted long after the lack of scientific justification should have been recognized."

But we know better now, which means that no matter how bad your back may be hurting, you'll be a whole lot better off to keep moving—if not actually walking around, then trying hard.

There's no trick at all to using crutches; anybody can learn the main points first time out. It takes only a couple of days to make a real expert of a learner, meaning a guy who can get across a room on crutches twice as fast as anybody with just his own two legs to depend on.

The body weight is carried almost entirely on the hands, arms and shoulders, relieving the aching back area of all strain and most, if not all, of the pain.

It is no exaggeration, and no idle talk, to say that exercise and diet together are two of the greatest factors in the physical welfare of the human being. Beyond anything else in the health picture, exercise and diet are entirely dependent on the voluntary effort and good sense of the patient.

Nobody else can take the exercise you should have, nor eat the things you should eat. It's straight do-it-yourself.

Unfortunately, pretty nearly all of us have been hearing about exercise and diet so long that both have joined the weather as something everybody talks about and nobody does anything about. That's especially bad because our twentieth century has set up an environment in which we survive by a push-button pattern of living, deliberately aimed at the elimination of physical exercise. The result has been to make exercise and diet more vitally important to your health than ever before.

This doesn't mean that you'd better rush off to the nearest gym and start throwing a medicine ball around. But it most certainly means that if you want to get the most out of being alive, you'd better get going with some reasonable exercise and pay a little more attention to your waist line.

There's no sense making it tough on yourself, either. To some extent, it's actually possible for you to exercise without so much as moving out of your chair. You can even get some healthy exercise lying in bed.

As for diet, there's one simple, easily understood bit of advice that can do more for your general health than the best calorie-counting program ever put together.

STOP NIBBLING!

For a starter, let's take a look at TV.

There you are, comfortably sprawled in your favorite easy chair, nicely relaxed and enjoying the entertainment. There's a glass of beer handy, or maybe milk, along with a big bowl of crisp, tasty potato chips.

169

Of course there'll be commercials, because somebody has to pay those performers you're watching, and you oughtn't to mind them too much. But whether you like them or not, you're going to get them, and for your armchair exercise they're just the thing.

Try this.

Every time the commercial comes on, you just take a deep breath and tighten up on those big, important abdominal

muscles of yours. Pull that sagging belly in as hard as you can while you mentally count fifteen. Then exhale and forget it until the commercial comes on again.

That's all. You don't have to work on anything else. And above all, don't fling back your shoulders, because all you do with that is to put a lot of unnecessary tension on some muscles of your upper back. If you can remember to stay with it for as little as six months, supposing you are an average TV fan, you'll begin to get results.

While you tie in your muscle-building with the TV commercials, you can make some major progress toward straightening out your diet problem, too. Just keep your fingers out of those potato chips. Better yet, don't even have them on hand, or any of the salted peanuts, crackers, or pretzels you've been munching in time to the music.

It might also be a good idea to quit sipping that beer, highball, or glass of milk. This kind of random, unnecessary eating and drinking, including those bedtime snacks and between-times candy bars, cookies, and tasty tidbits, represents the biggest part of our national overweight problem.

Cut them out, and you've come a long way toward better health.

The TV sit-down exercise program goes two ways. It's aimed at your general improvement, and it's directly intended to give your back a better chance.

In the first place, that sagging, pendulous pot some of us lug around is just so much extra dead weight for the working parts of the body to carry, a useless burden adding an extra load on the heart. Worse yet, by its very location it puts a special, extra strain on the lower back—the part of the back most likely to develop an ache. Likewise, that potbelly pulls the vital digestive system—stomach, intestines, and related abdominal organs—out of their proper position.

Stretched out of shape and pulled out of position by the

constant downward drag of that heavy overlay of useless fat, any one of these affected visceral organs can develop trouble —the kind of trouble turning up time after time in the form of one of those "referred cause" back pains mentioned in Chapter 7.

Requiring only a bit of gumption and determination, the little armchair exercise routine will slowly, but nonetheless surely, restore tone and function and usefulness to those flabby, tired, and long-neglected abdominal muscles. Once more they will be doing the job they were intended to do, the important job of providing proper support for the delicate internal organs located amidships in the human anatomy.

The office worker too, the fellow who is chained to a desk all day, can get a worthwhile measure of self-help merely through the persistent application of a few basic principles, easily and conveniently integrated with his job routine.

For one thing, the desk cowboy can cultivate good posture while seated at his work. It's a simple enough matter to sit in close, feet flat on the floor, with the spine as straight as possible, bringing the shoulders directly over the hips. That little lady sitting with one foot demurely tucked under her may look cute enough to slow down the boys a little, but she isn't doing her back any good.

Some of that TV abdominal-muscle training will also fit in very nicely with the office telephone. Every time it rings, let that be your reminder to tighten up your pudgy middle, if only for a few seconds. When you've repeated it often enough, the habit will become fixed, and you'll remember without the TV commercial or phone-bell reminder.

Actually, this is one of the best health habits you are ever likely to get: the all-important matter of keeping your tummy pulled in until the effort it costs you pays off. The payoff will be the development of well-conditioned abdominal muscles strong enough to hold all of your internal organs in their proper position.

Of course—and let's hope it just isn't so—you may be just so far gone by now that such a light, easy routine may require too much time to get you back into shape. In that case, you'll just have to look the trouble right in the eye and do something drastic. You'll have to stop fooling around with the easy way and go after the trouble the hard way, which means you are headed for some regular, vigorous, and comparatively strenuous exercise.

So let's get to it.

For equipment you're going to need nothing more than a little open space on your living room or bedroom floor, with or without carpet. There are three top-rate exercises which will bring quick results provided you are willing to invest a little physical effort in your health. These are the "Standing Bend-Over," the "Swinging Sit-Up," and the "Rocker."

The easiest of the lot is the "Standing Bend-Over." To do it, stand perfectly erect, heels together with the palms of your

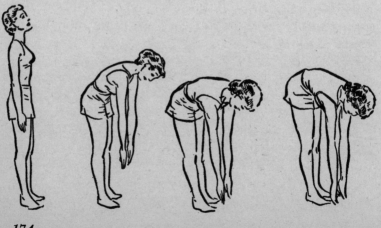

hands close to your sides. It's also a good idea to make sure you're clear of furniture directly in front of you. Now, bending from the hips and allowing the spine to curve forward carry both hands down toward the floor as far as you can go —and then some. If you can't get your hands lower than your knees WITHOUT BENDING YOUR KNEES, you're in bad shape for sure. If you can't, don't blame it on your belly. You're inability to do better means just one thing: the big "hamstring" muscles running from your buttocks down the back of your legs to a point just below the knee have lost their all-important elasticity. Likewise, the major muscles of your lower back associated with the hamstrings have become spastic, stiff, and generally out of physiological tune.

The exercise you are working on, provided you're working hard enough, will restore them to a healthy condition. It's all right to start off easy with, let's say, ten bend-overs. It isn't necessary to strain too much to begin with but—and this is important—you'll have to stay with it daily, increasing the effort each day, until one day you ought to wind up a standing bend-over with the tips of your fingers within an inch or two of the floor.

For the bend-over, gravity will be working for you but it's a different proposition in the "Swinging Sit-Up," in which gravity will be contributing a lot toward giving you a much harder time. In return for the hard time you'll be getting some hard, firm, and really useful muscles around your midriff. For a bonus, you will also be adding more flexibility and suppleness to those hamstrings and lower-back muscle mentioned before.

It begins easy enough—just stretch out on your back flat on the floor with your hands at your sides, heels together. Now it gets a little harder, because again WITHOUT BENDING YOUR KNEES try to swing straight up into a sitting position. About ten trys daily ought to do it. For once the specialists

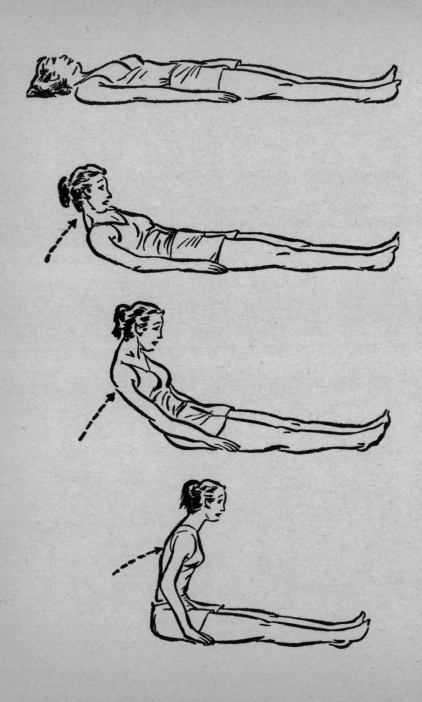

who planned these things are willing to concede a little something. If you need it at the start, and you probably will, it's perfectly all right and not considered cheating to help yourself up a little by pressing your hands and elbows against the floor. Extreme cases will scarcely be able to get their heads off the floor to begin with. It may call for a lot of persistent, regular, and honest effort to master the "Swinging Sit-Up," but the end results, in as little as three months perhaps, will be well worth it.

Like the "Swinging Sit-Up," you begin the "Rocker" by stretching out flat on the floor, this time face down. Hands at the sides and heels together as usual. Here, the big idea is to arch the back so that both head and feet come clear of the floor at the same time. Once more, DO NOT BEND THE KNEES. An expert rocker-man can finally wind up with his body in a perfect arc from forehead to toe, resting on a small portion of his mid-section only. If he's extra good he can actually rock a little, but such ability is hard to attain. There's only one way to do it—work.

The "Rocker" is designed solely to strengthen the back muscles.

The daily program should include a *minimum* of ten tries at each exercise, because all three are needed to achieve the best results. The "Standing Bend-Over," for instance, produces flexibility only. The "Swinging Sit-Up" gives both flexibility and strength, while the "Rocker" is planned simply to give greater strength.

The daily program should not take more than ten minutes, although beginners may require more time at first.

There's another helpful do-it-yourself idea around—let's call it a bit of negative exercise. By any name, this one can be a tremendous help for desk-bound people. In the long run it just might prevent development of a chronic, low-grade backache in the upper portion, between the shoulders.

The procedure is simplicity in itself, merely the conscious dropping of the shoulders from time to time.

It's easy—almost too easy to seem as important as it really is. Actually, it represents a direct and highly practical application of a relatively new idea in the rapidly expanding science of calisthenics and physical therapy. We now know that some occupations—desk jobs like typing, comptometer work, and driving for extended periods, for example—have a tendency to induce harmful muscle tensions in the upper-back area included in the "shoulder girdle."

A typist, for instance, unconsciously comes to elevate the shoulders, to "hunch up" more or less. This goes on day after day. The cumulative effect is harmful. Those unnecessarily tensed, tightened muscles, continuously under strain, begin to ache. In time, the ache becomes chronic. Its the kind of backache anybody can easily avoid just by remembering to let those shoulder muscles fall into their normal, relaxed condition as often as possible.

This doesn't mean squaring the shoulders army style. This may look just fine on Her Majesty's guardsmen on duty at Buckingham Palace. But physiologically it's all wrong. All it does for your back and shoulder muscles is to set up the same kind of useless tension you're trying to escape—only in another direction. Don't do it.

Along with your desk and favorite TV chair, your bed also can be a very fine place to work in some splendid exercise designed to strengthen your back.

It goes without saying that strong, well-conditioned back and stomach muscles are a big help in cutting down your chances of backache, especially of the kind induced by simple strain. And so it's well worth anybody's while to consider what can be done about your back to avoid the possibility

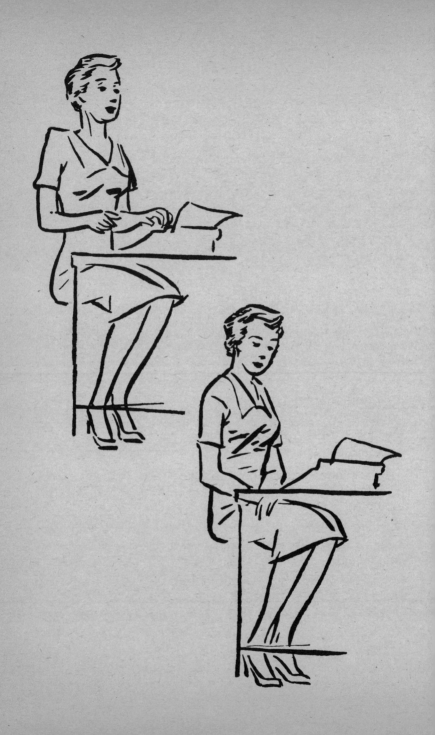

of winding up in the same bed trying to do something about a backache.

For a starter, you might give that good old sack of yours a critical once-over.

The bedstead ought to be well built and stable. The underlying spring system should be evenly supported, without bulges or hollows, topped by a firm, resilient mattress. The mattress needn't be some sort of a modified concrete slab, either. It should have just enough give to ensure even, comfortable bracing against the weight of your body. If you've been going along with some saggy, baggy pallet on the general theory that it's "well broken-in," get rid of it.

That hollow down the middle isn't a snug snoozing-slot home-tailored just for you, as might be supposed. Actually, its just a softly padded mantrap restricting the natural movements you should make while asleep.

Get rid of that beat-up bed.

After all, you're due to spend about a third of your time in it, so why not have it right? As a bonus, you'll get a private and first-class exercise platform for a few deceptively simple but enormously valuable in-bed movements anybody can manage.

Here's one. Stretch out, face up, legs extended, arms straight down and flat on the mattress. Now, still keeping the knees together, raise them until the soles of the feet are almost flat against the mattress. Now try to bring your head and one knee together, keeping your other leg and your arms in place. You won't make it—at least not at first—so just put the foot down again and drop the head.

Now do it again, this time with the other knee.

You won't score much better with the second knee, either. Now it's time to try both knees together, and anybody who

can do this one right off is excused, because the exercise isn't needed.

But for most of us, it's the other way around.

This being the case, for lazy people—which of course means most people—that little head-knee exercise just outlined is ideal. There's no need to get rough about it. Just take it easy—three, four, or five tries at each of the three movements will do for a starter. Gradually, this should be stepped up until you can run through the routine ten, fifteen, or even twenty times. At that point, you'll find a number of things have happened, all of them good.

You'll be feeling better all round because you'll be in better shape generally. Specifically, your chances of escaping a strain-type backache will be much, much better. The big psoas muscles, the main work horses in your back, and those important leg muscles called the hamstrings, will be strong, supple, and in top shape for their job. The major stomach muscles, called rectus abdominis, will be in condition to support any corporation you may still be carrying.

For a relatively small effort, it's a real buy at bargain-basement prices. But remember, regularity and sustained effort are important. After all, you can't expect to get something for nothing at all.

For those really determined people who mean business, there's another exercise that pays off very well indeed, considering the main drawback. For this one, unhappily, you'll just have to get on your feet and exercise standing up. No easy chair, no bed. Even so, it's far from strenuous. As a matter of fact, with this exercise you stand perfectly still. That's all.

All you have to do is stand up, but—here's the catch—you stand up in a very special way. You stand up absolutely straight. Before anybody gets to thinking that this is easy, it must be said that standing up absolutely straight is something nobody in the world does, at least not naturally. Nor should we, except for this exercise.

That's because in the normal, relaxed standing position, the human spine viewed sidewise runs in a long, gentle reverse curve.

The section of the whole curve we are most interested in right now begins at about the first lumbar vertebra, located about a hand span above the hips. It's an inward bend, ending at or near the fifth lumbar vertebra, just a little below the top of the hip bones.

This, then, is the curve which makes the small of your back. On a horse, if it is too deep, the nag is sway-backed. On a normal human, it is ordinarily just deep enough to allow you to slip your flattened hand into this hollow, between your back and any wall you might be leaning against.

Incidentally, a wall is the only piece of equipment you'll need for this bit of motionless exercise. Any nice smooth wall strong enough to stand a little solid pushing without falling down will do. A wall without a baseboard is best.

Put your shoulders against it as flat as possible. Your buttocks, the calves of your legs, and your heels, planted close together, should touch it also. Now you're all set for the big push—an attempt to narrow down that gap between the wall and the small of your back. It's to be done without allowing any part of you already in contact—shoulders, calves or heels —to lose that contact.

You'll quickly find out that you won't be able to close the gap entirely at first, not unless you're a trained gymnast and have been practicing. You'll also find out that after a while you can do it. You'll be able to close that gap completely, bringing your whole spinal column from shoulders to hips into an entirely straight line, and hold it there for as long as you like.

The pull set up by this flat-wall process again goes right into those stomach and back muscles mentioned before, the ones which can contribute so much to over-all good health, and more yet to a strong, trouble-free back. For a bonus, you'll develop healthy, flexible, sound conditions in the small, all-important muscles and ligaments directly involved with your spine and its tremendously vital intervertebral disks. Moreover, the improvement will be greatest right where it is needed the most—in the lumbar area. It's a lot for a little.

All of the foregoing can't possibly pretend to represent more than an irreducible minimum of the countless exercises available for various purposes, including back-strengthening. But each exercise outlined is convenient, simple, and above all useful. Despite their apparently trifling nature, they can and do work wonders.

As a matter of fact, there are all kinds of helpful exercises your doctor may suggest, even though you may already be stretched out with a bad back. Naturally, the proper exercise advisable for a particular condition depends on the individual case.

The whole question of muscular movement presents one more example of the wondrous way in which the human body is organized to serve our ends. The entirely automatic synchronization, because of which in health each and every muscle of our bodies can relax or tighten in perfect coordination to perform the simplest movement, is in itself a true marvel of living mechanics. The right kind of physical exercise can maintain and improve every muscle capacity you have, as well as restore many you may have lost.

For our times, a Swedish gymnast named Per Henrik Ling

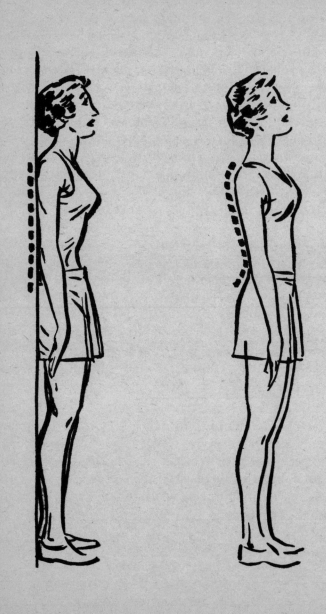

set the pace more than a century ago. Born in 1776, Ling was an author of considerable merit and a poet as well, but these sedentary side lines didn't interfere at all with his main occupation, which was teaching people how to have and keep sound, healthy bodies. Before he died in 1839, he'd been fencing master at the University of Lund in Sweden, and later at a military school in Karlsborg. After that, Ling, working with his son Hjalmar, set up his own gymnastic institute in Stockholm, where he developed the formalized muscle-building system which soon became the world-famous "Swedish Movements."

What Ling started is still going on, as any training-camp soldier struggling with push-ups, calisthenics, setting-up exercises and the like will ruefully testify. But no matter how much these rigorous, rhythmic routines may take out of him, they'll put a lot more back.

And so will the exercise-diet advice outlined in this chapter, but merely reading about what others can do won't do you much good.

You'll have to do it yourself.

18. STANDARD MISTREATMENTS

RIGHT NOW tremendous droves of utterly wretched human beings are being variously roasted, from the inside out, or the outside in, or the backside up—trussed up, sliced open, stretched out, and singed over.

And these aren't hapless prisoners condemned to torture in some Bamboo Curtain concentration camp, either. On the contrary, these poor devils are being cared for tenderly by well-trained, solicitous uniformed attendants. Most often they are surrounded by anxiously sympathetic friends and relatives while they endure their fate with what fortitude they have. Each fondly anticipates a quick, happy return to his home and the bosom of his family.

Hospitals are loaded with pain-wracked people who ought to be well. Moreover, with just a little better understanding of the basic factors involved in low-back disorders, by far the most of them might have been spared hospitalization in the first place. In the main, the history behind these needlessly hospitalized patients is the same, by and large.

They've all got bad backs of some kind; they've all tried first one thing and then another, and they've all finally ended up in the hospital in a last-ditch, all-out effort to lick the misfortune that's been licking them.

With the kindest intentions in the world the hospital is sincerely trying to help—patiently, faithfully, conscientiously applying the good old stand-by procedures they've always used. The doctors, nurses, orderlies, and everybody else, including the elevator operators and the superintendent, are doing their best.

But these patients we're talking about aren't getting well. Weeks, months, sometimes even years go on, and so do these luckless people, wearily fighting a hopeless battle. They've tried anything and everything. As likely as not, many of them have shopped around before coming into the hospital, vainly plodding the rounds from doctor to doctor, hopefully trying first this and then that, and clearly getting nowhere except maybe a little older, a little more discouraged, and a whole lot unhappier.

Others have doggedly stuck it out with some hard-working family physician with about the same result. Far too many of those bad backs never get any better. They could and should get better, and here's how and why.

In the last analysis, except for a relatively small percentage of cases, there is scarcely any variety of backache that will not respond to just four therapeutic measures. Each is available to any physician. He needn't be a specialist, and what simple techniques may be needed are easily acquired.

They are rest, sclerotherapy, curare, and a few well-established osteopathic manipulations. The solution to almost any low-back problem is just that simple.

Of course, your general health is highly important, as it is in the treatment of any ailment, and so your over-all condition must be given a thorough going-over, which it ought to be getting at all times anyhow.

But it is now abundantly plain that there are any number of treatments in common use, the so-called standard treatments, which on the basis of the record must be classified once and for all as being of dubious value at best, if not actually harmful. To put it bluntly, they just aren't any good.

The list includes some long-established therapeutic fixtures like traction, body casts, braces, the weirdly conceived procedure called "nerve stretching," diathermy, disk operations, and most bone grafts.

In short, the major stand-bys now in use.

Briefly, and as a matter of statistics if nothing else, any back case apparently improved by these methods could have been much more improved, and perhaps entirely cured at a far smaller cost in pain, time, and money—not to mention far less risk.

Of all the pseudoscientific booby traps around, traction is beyond all doubt the worst. This traction business is a form of treatment frequently used in herniated-disk cases, acute low-back strain, or low-back muscular disorders in general. In it, the patient is put in a fracture bed—a springless pallet of tightly-stretched canvas surmounted by a rectangular framework of metal pipe. This framework supports a trapezelike swinging bar suspended by ropes so that it dangles above the patient just about over his chest.

With the patient stretched flat on his back, another ingenious arrangement of ropes and pulleys permits the attachment of weights to the patient's legs to exert a downward pull. The weights run anywhere from five to fifteen pounds. By heaving on the trapeze, the patient can shift himself around a little now and then to ease his general discomfort.

This peculiar device is called Buck's extension, after a certain Dr. Gurdon Buck who developed the rig back in 1860 as an aid in the treatment of fractured legs. However, when used to treat a herniated disk, the idea is that the vertebrae at the point of damage will be pulled apart, widening the space between them, and thereby relieving the pressure on the collapsed disk in question. Which in turn is supposed to relieve the pain more effectively than merely lying in bed.

All this is just fine, except that Dr. Sanford R. Rothenberg, who made one of the most thorough and scientific investigations of traction on record, was unable to find anything of the sort. He said so in his official report presented in the May, 1953, issue of *Surgery, Gynecology and Obstetrics.*

Five patients under traction for ruptures of lumbar intervertebral disks, the common "slipped disk," were checked for the supposed separation, or pulling apart, right down to the last fraction of an inch. Dr. Rothenberg's method was simplicity in itself—the kind of simplicity that amounts to genius. He performed an exploratory operation on each of the five, laying bare the affected area to permit the taking of direct, positive measurements. Obviously, since each patient was under the necessary operative anaesthesia, unaffected by spasmodic tension or conscious reaction of any kind, the traction to be applied could produce its best effect, if any.

The distance between each vertebra was measured. Then the traction weights were hooked up, and the same measurements taken again.

With five, or with fifteen pounds, or even with an unheard-of fifty-pound pull, there was absolutely no separation of the vertebrae such as is supposed to occur. None.

The space between those vertebra remained exactly the same, with or without the weights. The report should have put an end to the solemn myth that traction can ease vertebral pressure on a damaged disk, or an undamaged one for that matter. But firmly imbedded notions, however mistaken, have a habit of hanging on; so traction survives sense, and its victims survive somehow.

Furthermore, Dr. Rothenberg found there was absolutely no indication of any relaxation of the back muscles, which it was thought traction was producing.

191

In short, if Dr. Rothenberg's demonstration did nothing else it served to offer irrefutable scientific proof of something any patient under traction knows as a matter of bitter experience.

But traction in one form or another has been around for a long time, which may be one reason why it hangs on. For a fact, the prototype of the modern traction device goes back to medieval times, when Guy de Chauliac, a French physician, developed what was known as the Balkan frame. As he himself described it in *Collectio Chirurgia Venetia*, printed in Venice in 1519, the Balkan frame is to all intents and purposes the same traction device in use today.

As with all the problems everybody must meet and somehow solve, what not to do is likely to be just as important as anything else. The don'ts rank with the dos, and if the problem is about your back, one particular don't towers miles above every other consideration in the picture.

Don't have anything to do with traction!

As a reasonable backache treatment, body casts make just as little sense. Therapeutically, they are logically in the same class with the more frequently used body-strapping method, in which the torso is merely bound around with strips of adhesive tape—except that the body cast is much more impressive and also heavier. Braces of one sort or another are also frequently tried. These are generally cumbersome contraptions of leather-padded steel, held in place by either laces or buckles. All are based on the same notion.

Supported by the back and lower torso, to which they are applied, they are supposed to support the back and lower torso. The idea is in the same category as a man hoisting himself up by his own bootstraps. Aside from the galling, chafing, and irritation they often produce, neither the cast, nor the strapping, nor the harness can do a thing except limit or restrain normal back motion.

And to the extent that this occurs, they must inevitably serve only to accelerate the weakening and atrophy that comes to any muscle or joint after long disuse. At best, they represent a temporizing compromise with some kind of an operation. They cannot cure. The wasting away and deterioration of otherwise healthy muscles that can be caused by such devices is both shocking and needless, and the inescapable constriction of circulation their use sets up is certainly dangerous to over-all health.

Now let's have a look at "nerve stretching," a procedure often used in an effort to deal with sciatica.

Before the advent of this variety of therapeutic nonsense, any schoolboy who'd as much as skimmed through his physiology book could explain that muscle tissue, and muscle tissue only, comprises the only part of your body that can alter shape, which is essentially what your muscles do when they contract or expand again to their normal relaxed position. Bone, cartilage, and similar components of the human body can neither stretch nor contract. Most certainly nerve tissue, in the sciatic nerves as well as all others, can't.

Nevertheless, nerve stretching still goes on.

To do it, the affected leg is forcibly straightened out from hip to ankle, after which the leg is encased in a cast to hold it straight up in the air as the patient lies flat on his back. The job is done under anaesthesia.

To be sure, until then the patient will instinctively ease the pain by lying on his good side, with the aching leg pulled up in a half-bent position with the knee partly flexed. While the nerve stretching is under way, the leg is held in a completely unnatural position, as anybody can easily determine by trying it out.

Actually, the effort is specifically aimed at stretching the hamstrings a little, which, since they are muscle tissue, can of course be truly stretched to some degree. And also of course, the very first chance they get, which would be the moment the cast is chopped away, these muscles promptly snap back again where they were to begin with.

The sciatic nerve remains unchanged in any way, and in all likelihood, the real cause of the pain as well as the pain itself does the same.

Diathermy, in the pathology of the lower back, is just about as common as it is useless. True enough, diathermy is easy to apply and easy to take, and may induce a temporary warm and cozy feeling easily mistaken for actual relief of pain; but that's as far as it goes. For a certainty, diathermy, no matter how often applied, is no cure. Diathermy is just so much wasted time, effort, and money, and reliance on it can well delay the proper treatment to the patient's ultimate disadvantage.

There is no therapeutic mystery about diathermy despite the impressive dials, switches, and soothing hum of the electric machine used to produce it. In principal, the diathermic machine can't do a thing that a well-placed hot-water bottle or electric heating pad can't do with a lot less fuss. Except that the machine is supposed to generate heat more deeply in the tissue, the general idea is the same—to induce a concentration of blood in the affected area by dilating, or expanding, the blood vessels involved, for what that may be worth.

Actually, such mere concentration of blood for the duration of the treatment is relatively meaningless. It is by circulation, rather than by its mere presence, that the blood stream accomplishes its work in the body, and no amount of diathermy is capable of altering circulation in any significant way, least of all permanently.

Some conclusions reached in 1950 by Dr. Joseph L. Hollander, head of the Arthritis Clinic at the University of Pennsylvania School of Medicine, are revealing as to the over-all effectiveness of mere heat, deep or any other kind. Dr. Hollander dealt specifically with painful knee joints, but his results can be easily extended to include all muscular pain.

Using delicate thermometers deeply imbedded in the tissue, Dr. Hollander established beyond question that the more heat present above normal body temperature, the more these joints hurt and the stiffer they got. The more closely normal body temperature was maintained, the less pain and soreness followed. So much for diathermy.

There's another variety of heat treatment sometimes prescribed in this medical age of enlightenment that smells like something right out of a first-class medieval torture chamber. It is mentioned here only to show how plain, ordinary therapeutic horse sense can occasionally be drowned out by certain schools of scientific silliness.

This involves actual scorching of the flesh with an electric cautery as a "counter-irritant" to sciatica, as if the pain of the burn added to the pain of the sciatica would add up to no pain at all. Fortunately it isn't often used, probably because few patients will hold still for it, even if somebody is goofy enough to suggest it. It belongs in the same class as the bee-sting treatment.

Aside from this, then, traction, body casts, braces, the so-called nerve stretching, and diathermy remain as the mainstays of the conservative measures generally recommended for better or worse. Too often it results in the latter, whereupon the next resort is to the radical procedures, or surgery.

There are several types of operations, all delicate and none certain, available. The disk operation, or laminectomy, performed to relieve the slipped or herniated disk, is the more common.. It is often supplemented by another technique called arthrodesis, at once or perhaps later.

Through an incision along the line of the spine, the affected disk is laid bare, and the core of the disk, the nucleus pulposus, is scooped out with a curette, a surgical instrument used like a scraper. This simply amounts to removing this injured part entirely, like an unwanted appendix. The surgeon may then proceed to bolster the weakened spinal column by screwing the adjacent vertebrae together. Small pilot holes are drilled through the upper and lower vertebral facets, after which a couple of strong screws, made of some chemically inert metal like Vitallium, are driven home. This is called arthrodesis.

Naturally the vertebral joint they've screwed up ceases to exist. But the statistics cited earlier prove that too often the trouble doesn't. No competent carpenter would approve of the poor mechanical principle by which these screws are supposed to bear the burden imposed upon them. At best, a lucky patient can expect to get by with a back that, while it may not give actual pain, will certainly never be normal again.

There remains finally the matter of certain bone-grafting techniques.

As to their use in sacroiliac cases, little more need be said, but in connection with laminectomy, bone grafts are sometimes substituted for arthrodesis. One method works about as well as the other. Bone grafts used to fuse the adjacent vertebrae after laminectomy, like those grafts previously mentioned which are used to provide greater stability for a weakened sacroiliac, are no bargain even in a free hospital.

Such, by and large, is the nature of your back and its afflictions.

Eons of biological development and structural evolution have made it what it is today—a vitally important and wonderfully fine framework for your marvelous body. Treat it well and it will serve you well.

And if trouble moves in on you in spite of everything,

don't let a bad back get you down spiritually, even though you may be physically floored. Now is the time to hang on to your well-known sunny disposition, paste a smile on your face even if the lips will tremble a little, and fight back. Any kind of a smile helps, even a forced one.

Remember that you are not alone, that help is at hand, and your chances of getting yourself a better back grow better every day.

The medical wisdom of centuries, the last hard-won advances of modern experimental science, the sincere and dedicated services of trained, resourceful and conscientious physicians are yours to command.

And finally, there's still more help for you, the big help that a barber's apprentice turned surgeon, and one of the all-time greats among the world's healers, learned about on the battlefields of France four hundred years ago. To this day the medical art of mankind has evolved no greater or more enduring truth than Ambroise Paré knew then.

"I dressed his wounds," he humbly declared, "and God healed him."

APPENDIX: FOR DOCTORS ONLY

MEMBERS OF the medical profession who are fond of the antiquities will readily recall what appears to be the earliest technical reference to sclerotherapy as such, found in Hippocrates' dissertation *On the Articulations.*

As a matter of modern practice, its use can be said to date from the initial injections reported by Valpeau in 1835. Present techniques for unstable joints, dating from 1937, have been largely developed by the work of Dr. Earl H. Gedney, D.O., former chief surgeon at Bangor Osteopathic Hospital, Bangor, Maine.

Sclerotherapy is favorably indicated in the treatment of hypermobile knee, recurrent shoulder dislocations, and hypermobile temporomandibular articulation, and is recommended also as the therapy of choice in the management and improvement of hypermobile sacroiliacs, unstable zygapophysials, uncompensated degenerated disk, and spondylolisthesis.

The needles required are those ordinarily used in general practice, with the possible exception of the three- or four-inch varieties, in either 19 or 20 gauge. The choice of a long or short bevel is, as elsewhere, a matter of personal preference. Of the solutions, Sylnosol, (Searle, Chicago) or Alparene No.

198

2 (Dequin Physician's Products Co., Chicago) have been proven satisfactory. Others are available.

It becomes increasingly apparent that some hitherto generally accepted concepts relative to the etiology of pain from the uncompensated degenerated intervertebral disk can no longer be regarded as reasonably tenable.

The adequacy of the currently popular theory that indiscriminately attributes established sciatic neuritis to a radiculitis attendant upon retropulsive herniation of the nucleus pulposus, must be radically revised in the light of recent nucleographical evidence. Likewise, considerable significance must be given to the increasing frequency with which arthrodesis has been necessarily offered as supplementary procedure following laminectomy.

The appearance of extensive deterioration of the annulus fibrosus is not inevitably indicative of or accompanied by either posterior or postero-lateral bulging against proximate nerve roots, nor can the desirability of postoperative results achieved by laminectomy alone be expected to compare with those possible when both laminectomy and arthrodesis are performed.

In passing, the radical content found in this type of surgery must receive serious consideration, and recourse to either or both operative procedures should be properly postponed in favor of any available and less drastic response to the diagnosis, such as adequate sclerotherapy, for instance.

The investigations of Lindblom and Hultquist clearly demonstrate that normal absorption can, with considerable certainty, be relied upon to clear the nucleus pulposus. Subsequent development of supportive fibrous tissue, or complete bony ankylosis may ensue. In any case, a natural re-establishment of stability, minus of course, the normal nuclear hydrodynamic cushion, is ordinarily observable.

The therapeutic philosophy of sclerotherapy contemplates

the logical and benign stimulation of the natural formation of such supportive fibrous tissue as noted by Lindblom and Hultquist, by the introduction hypodermically of a few well-established and thoroughly tested solutions designed to accelerate this process.

A brief résumé of techniques may be useful and in order at this point, beginning with the treatment of the classic uncompensated degenerated intervertebral disk in recogni-

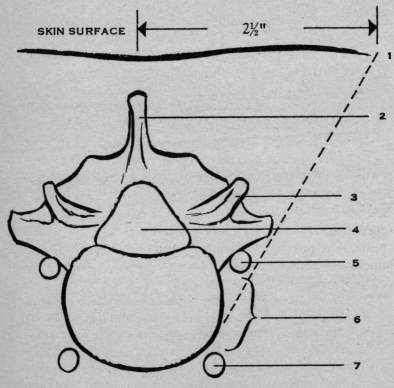

DISK TECHNIQUE

1. Point of insertion. 2. Spinous process. 3. Transverse process. 4. Spinal canal. 5. Nerve root. 6. Injection site. 7. Blood vessels and sympathetics.

tion of the comparative importance of this condition among those to whom sclerotherapy is adapted.

With the lumbo-pelvic area suitably exposed, the patient is placed upon the table prone. The table-break is then adjusted to obliterate the normal lumbar curve. Where the table in use does not include a break, a firm pillow or similar support introduced under the abdominal area is an acceptable substitute.

A similar disposal of the patient is also made in the treatment of hypermobile sacroiliac, unstable zygapophyseals, and spondylolisthesis.

Preliminary roentgenological evaluation of the lumbar spine and pelvis, as determined by antero-posterior, and lateral views plus right and left oblique views made in the recumbent position, with a supplemental antero-posterior plate made in the erect position, is essential. Additionally, such study frequently facilitates the accurate establishment of the surgical landmarks to be observed.

The usual aseptic precautions applicable are carried out. The injections are administered bilaterally.

An initial injection of .5 cc. procaine, 2 per cent, is made subcutaneously at the site using a one-half inch, 27 gauge needle. The proper site is found 5 cm. lateral to the interspinous space at the proximate level of the involved intervertebral disk.

With anesthesia effected, the physician may then proceed with a four-inch needle, 19 or 20 gauge. The needle is directed anteriorly and medially to slightly impinge upon the disk, anterior to the adjacent nerve roots.

The utmost caution must be exercised in this passage of the needle to ensure accurate placement of the sclerosing solution.

In particular, insertion made too vertically may result in the accidental puncture of either the aorta or the vena cava,

201

both of which lie anterior to the lumbar vertebrae at this point. On the other hand, direction along a too horizontal line may project the needle tip into adjacent nerve roots.

Likewise, an excessively cephalad route risks encounter with the transverse process of the vertebra immediately above, while a corresponding misdirection caudad may similarly strike the transverse process of the vertebra immediately below. The impingement of the needle into the annulus fibrosus becomes manifest when the characteristic toughness of this tissue, as compared with mere muscle tissue, is felt. Routine aspiration is then indicated.

Injection of the solution, usually .2 cc., is then completed. However, it is of extreme importance that exact insertion of the needle has been accomplished before injection is made, otherwise the procedure is, of course, entirely ineffective.

In spondylolisthesis, the technique is exactly similar, except that placement of the solution is made at the annulus fibrosus both above and below the anteriorly displaced vertebra.

In either condition, adequate response may be anticipated in from eight to ten treatments.

Obviously, many of the above remarks, such as those concerning the roentgenological surveys indicated and other data, apply likewise to sclerotherapy of the hypermobile sacroiliac, except that the anesthetic preparation indicated for the deeper areas previously involved may here be dispensed with in nearly all instances.

The convenient needle, depending upon the general conformation of the patient, is either a two-inch, 22 gauge, or a three-inch, 20 gauge. Insertion is made approximately 1.25 cm. medial to the posterior superior iliac spine, being directed laterally and anteriorly thereunder up to the sacroiliac ligaments. These lie variously at depths ranging from 2.5 to 7.5 cm. Sharply increased resistance to further needle

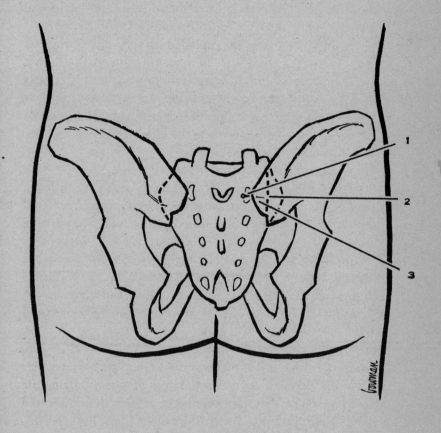

SACROILIAC INJECTION
1. Point of insertion. 2. Sacroiliac joint. 3. Posterior, superior
iliac spine.

pressure plainly establishes attainment of the proper depth in any given instance.

As in most other spinal procedures, sclerotherapeutic approaches to hypermobile sacroiliac are carried out bilaterally, with dosages running from a minimal injection of .3 cc. up to a maximal 1 cc. As with problems arising from degenerative disk complaints, approximately eight to ten treatments should suffice to secure substantial improvements. In especially felicitous circumstances, measurable improvement may sometimes be noted in as few as three, or possibly four, treatments.

If, as rarely happens, no noticeable betterment is observable after a reasonable period, further sources of irritation, such as possible and previously undetected disk aspects, or conceivably adverse zygapophyseal conditions should be investigated.

In the diagnosis of zygapophyseal developmental anomalies —obliquity, sagittal-coronal facings, and rudimentary articular surfaces—the right and left oblique lumbar roentgenological views previously described in discussing herniated disks are mandatory. These conditions and the consequent instability occur most frequently in L 4 and L 5.

As a matter of technique, the landmark here is precisely the same as in the disk procedure, the ideal needle being the two-inch, 22 gauge. Insertion, normally without anesthesia, is made 1.25 cm. laterally, anteriorly, and penetration effected to depths of from 2.5 cm. to 4 cm. to reach the capsular ligaments of the facets.

Naturally, injection is performed bilaterally, and, in sclerotherapy generally, the anticipated duration of treatment scheduled weekly is from eight to ten weeks.

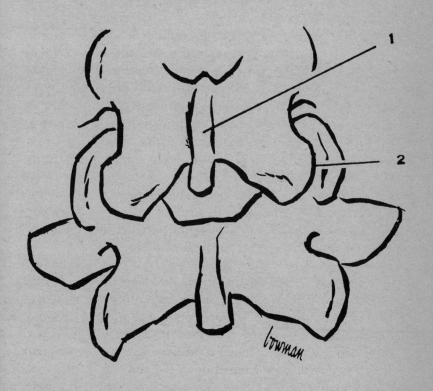

ZYGAPOPHYSEAL TECHNIQUE
1. Spinous process. 2. Zygapophyseal.

Therapeutic curare in the form of Tubadil, and certain other competitive products, is pharmaceutically classified with the alkaloids. As customarily prepared by Endo Products Company, New York, Tubadil is packaged in 5 cc. vials. It consists of a repository injection of tubocurarine chloride suspended in a peanut oil, oxycholesterol derivative and bees-wax menstruum.

Its use in shock therapy, manipulative procedures, and endoscopic techniques such as laryngoscopy, bronchoscopy, esophagoscopy, sigmoidoscopy, as well as in musculoskeletal disorders and neurological manifestations, is well established.

However, in view of its peculiar characteristics, a more extensive use of this drug by physicians generally should be seriously considered. This is especially the case in connection with classic acute low-back strain of traumatic etiology.

Under such conditions, the preparation has exceptional lissive value, and where indications of striated muscle spasm exist, it may be administered in dosages set forth in the accompanying table. The ideal is intragluteal administration. However, under adverse conditions, the deltoid or any similar muscle may be chosen. It must not be given intravenously.

The absolute contraindication is myasthenia gravis. The partial antidote is Prostigmin, 1 cc.–1/1000, while the absolute antidote is Tensilon, 1 cc. Both are by Hoffman La-Roche. Effective reactions lasting as much as twenty-four hours following injection have been observed. The active component of the repository mixture is properly and quickly destroyed soon after effective release, and repeated dosages have demonstrated a complete absence of inconvenient habit-forming propensities or comparable deficiencies.

Bennett, Fuller, Hoback, Jonez, and others have elsewhere discussed the uniformly satisfactory results obtained in treatment of various pathological entities such as dystonia, athetosis, cerebral plastic diplegia, tetanus, and multiple sclerosis.

DOSAGE SCHEDULE

PATIENT'S WEIGHT	MINIMUM DOSE	MAXIMUM DOSE
80 lbs.	.35 cc.	.65 cc.
90 lbs.	.40 cc.	.70 cc.
100 lbs.	.45 cc.	.80 cc.
110 lbs.	.50 cc.	.90 cc.
120 lbs.	.60 cc.	1.00 cc.
130 lbs.	.65 cc.	1.05 cc.
140 lbs.	.70 cc.	1.10 cc.
150 lbs.	.75 cc.	1.20 cc.
160 lbs.	.80 cc.	1.30 cc.
170 lbs.	.85 cc.	1.35 cc.
180 lbs.	.90 cc.	1.45 cc.
190 lbs.	.95 cc.	1.50 cc.
200 lbs.	1.05 cc.	1.60 cc.

and add .08 cc. for each additional 10 lbs. thereafter.

The principal effective manipulative techniques applicable to low-back maladies are relatively simple, conveniently executed, and significantly adequate. Those for general relaxation, sacroiliac adjustment, and lumbar correction will be described here. A suitable table of convenient height, adequately cushioned and preferably rather narrow is best. The back of the patient is exposed as required.

The first procedure, affording relaxation of the lumbar musculature in general, may be offered independently for its inherent value, or it may be given in conjunction with, and preliminary to, subsequent therapy of a more specific nature.

With the patient prone, the palmar surface of one hand,

reinforced by the other superimposed, is applied to the lumbar area on the selected side. Steady pressure, directed anteriorly and medially, is thereupon brought to bear, lightly at the outset and increasing gradually to a maximum. In this connection, some judgment must be exercised to apportion the maximum pressure used to the general stature, weight, age, and condition of the patient.

Ordinarily, the heaviest pressure of which the physician is capable may be exerted upon average adults.

Following firm retention for a few minutes, the pressure is gradually relaxed and reapplied with a rhythmic repetition over an approximate period of from five to six minutes. The technique is, of course, used bilaterally.

In the presence of spasm, and emphatically in the presence of acute spasm, the gradual release of the therapeutic pressure is imperative. Sudden release nullifies the effectiveness of the treatment and sharply aggravates the pain. The patient experiences a marked, momentary intensification of the pain, while the physician may actually feel a pronounced, spasmodic muscular contraction following such oversudden release.

The accepted technique indicated in the correction of sacroiliac lesion affords effective remedial rotation of the ilium, either posteriorly or anteriorly as may be required.

It is performed with the patient recumbent upon the side opposite to that under treatment. For present purposes, the immediate discussion contemplates treatment of the left sacroiliac articulation. There should be no difficulty in transposition of these remarks to include the contralateral side.

A flexure of approximately 30 degrees is made in both thighs, after which the left leg is permitted to drop unsupported over the table edge. The right arm, firmly grasped, is then extended upwards above the head, and sufficient tension exerted to induce considerable torsion in the spine.

This disposal of the patient effectively locks, or immobilizes

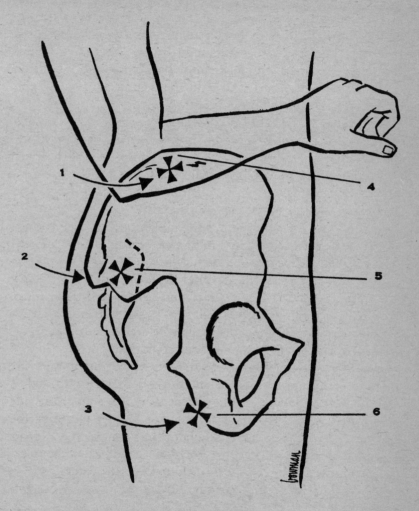

LUMBAR LESIONS

1. Arm thrusts in this direction for correction of posterior sacroiliac. 2. Arm thrusts in this direction for correction of lumbar lesion. 3. Arm thrusts in this direction for correction of anterior sacroiliac. 4. Crest of ilium. 5. Sacroiliac joint. 6. Tuberosity of ischium.

the vertebral column, principally through the consequent closer engagement of the zygapophyseals. The rigidity thus created is conducive to more efficient transmission along the column of subsequent therapeutical pressure.

Where the lesion is posterior, the physician's right forearm is brought to bear upon the crest of the ilium. If anterior, the forearm rests upon the ischial tuberosity. In either case, the left hand, with the arm fully extended, is placed firmly against the patient's left shoulder.

A sharp and firmly pronounced thrust is to be delivered through both arms simultaneously, posteriorly with the left hand, and anteriorly with the right.

In the adjustment of lumbar lesions, the technique is precisely similar to the foregoing with one exception. This relates to the placement of the physician's right forearm, here to be applied immediately above the sacroiliac articulation midpoint between the crest of the ilium and the ischial tuberosity.

The judicious use of an analgesic injection, such as procaine, for example, will readily occur to the practicing physician, and is recommended. A typical suggested dose, looking to the muscular infiltration indicated in fibrositis, for instance, might be 5 cc. or more as conditions may determine. In connection with sensory neutralization desired in nerve root involvements, zygapophysealic or sacroiliac sprains, and in the sciatic nerve as situated midway between the ischial tuberosity and the greater trochanter of the femur, smaller doses may suffice.

Finally, the increasingly manifest efficacy of direct mechanical equalization of divergent leg lengths plainly warrants wider acceptance by the medical profession generally. The condition is clearly responsible for much low-back distress due to attendant pathological inclination of the pelvis, commonly described as "pelvic tilt." The consequent compensatory lateral curvature of the spine which normally results is a well-understood source of considerable discomfort.

Such leg-length equalization as may be found necessary is conveniently achieved by the orthopedic adjustment of the patient's footwear as directed. The insertion of one or more supplementary layers of leather, generally ·called lifts, into the heel on one side, or conversely, proportionate removal from the other, or perhaps both measures, may be employed.

In dealing with the simplest situation possible, wherein the sacral base line displays pronounced inclination downward toward the shorter limb and the ensuing compensatory lumbar scoliosis is ipsilaterally convex, no particular difficulty is presented. The adjustment is made correspondingly, possibly by degrees if the patient is older or the lift required is somewhat greater than usual. Adjustments up to .6 cm. are not unusual.

However, contralateral scoliotic convexity may set up pathological complications of considerable intricacy, and should be approached with extreme caution. Fortunately the latter condition is relatively rare.

More frequent X-ray and clinical examination, augmented manipulative treatments, and possibly sclerotherapy, must be considered in these cases. Lifts employed may be experimentally introduced as in the ipsilateral situations.

A final word of caution may be appropriate. Conservatively, lifts are accurately prescribed only after careful roentgenological evaluation. The empirical approach offers many latent hazards, and cannot be recommended. The view taken antero-posteriorly in the erect position, embraces the lumbar spine and pelvis.

BIBLIOGRAPHY

I. MANIPULATION

STILL, A. T. *Philosophy and Mechanical Principles of Osteo-pathy.* Kansas City, Mo.: Hudson-Kimberly Pub. Co., 1902.

STILL, A. T. *Research and Practice.* Kirksville, Mo.: Published by the author, 1910.

SCHWAB, W. A. "Principles of Manipulative Treatment," *Journal of American Osteopathic Association,* Feb. and March, 1932.

GOLDTHWAIT, J. R. *Essentials of Body Mechanics in Health and Disease,* (4th ed.). Philadelphia: J. B. Lippincott Co., 1945.

STARKS, C. R. "Clinical Observations in Sciatica," *Journal of the American Osteopathic Association,* August, 1948.

CLYBOURNE, H. E. "Low-Back Problem," *Journal of the American Osteopathic Association,* Jan., 1947.

WRIGHT, J. "Mechanics in Relation to Derangement of Facet Joints of Spine," *Archives of Physical Therapy,* April, 1944.

MORTON, S. A. "Value of the Oblique View in the Radiographic Examination of the Lumbar Spine," *Radiology,* Nov., 1937.

HADLEY, L. A. "Subluxation of Apophyseal Articulations with Bony Impingement as Cause of Pain," *American Journal of Roentgenology,* Feb., 1953.

ZUKERMAN, A. G. "The Articular Facets and the Osteopathic Spinal Lesion," *Journal of the American Osteopathic Association,* Jan., 1950.

CHAMBERLAIN, W. E. "The Symphysis Pubis in the Roentgen Examination of the Sacroiliac Joint." Read at the 23rd meeting of the American Roentgen Ray Society, Los Angeles, September 12-16, 1923. *American Journal of Roentgen and Radium Therapy*, Dec., 1930.

COYER, A. B., and CURWEN, I. H. "Low Back Pain Treated by Manipulation; a Controlled Series," *British Medical Journal* #4915 (19 March, 1955), pp. 705-07.

LIEVRE, J. A. "Apropos des traitment des lombalgies et sciatique par les manipulation vertebrales" (Treatment of lumbar backache and sciatica by vertebral manipulation), *Revue des Rheumatisme et des Maladies Osteo-Articulares* (Paris), 22:9-10 (Sept.-Oct., 1955), pp. 651-6.

McCONVILLE, B. E. "Conservative Management of Low Back Pain," *American Journal of Surgery*, 85:3 (March, 1953), pp. 335-8.

MENSOR, MERRILL C. "Nonoperative Treatment Including Manipulation for Lumbar Intervertebral Disk Syndrome," *Journal of Bone and Joint Surgery*, Oct., 1955, 37A pp. 925.

II. JOINT SCLEROTHERAPY

HIPPOCRATES. *The Genuine Works of.* Translated by Francis Adams. Baltimore, Md.: Williams & Wilkins, 1946.

VALPEAU, A. A. L. M. *New Elements of Operative Surgery.* Translated by P. S. Townsend. Wood, N.Y.: 1847.

RICE, CARL O., and MATSON, H. "Histologic Changes in the Tissues of Man and Animals Following the Injection of Irritating Solutions Intended for the Cure of Hernia," *Illinois Medical Journal*, 70:271-78 (Sept., 1936).

GEDNEY, EARL H. "The Hypermobile Joint," *Osteopathic Profession*, June, 1937.

———. "Disk Syndrome," *ibid.*, Sept., 1951.

SHUMAN, DAVID. "Unstable Back," *Osteopathic Profession*, Sept., 1951.

————. "Technics for Treating Instability of the Joints by Sclerotherapy," *ibid.*, May, 1953.

COVENTRY, MARK B., GHORMLEY, RALPH K., and KERNOHAN, JAMES W. "The Intervertebral Disk: Its Microscopic Anatomy and Pathology," *Journal of Bone and Joint Diseases*, Jan., April, and July, 1945.

BRADFORD, F. K., and SPURLING, R. G. *The Intervertebral Disk* (2nd ed.). Springfield, Ill.: Charles C. Thomas, 1947.

LINDBLOM, K., and HULTQUIST, G. "Absorption of Protruded Disk Tissue," *Journal of Bone and Joint Surgery*, July, 1950.

LINDBLOM, K. "Technic and Results in Myelography and Disk Puncture," *Acta Radiologica* (Stockholm), Vol. 34 (Oct.-Nov., 1950), pp. 321-30.

ERLACHER, PETER R. "Nucleography," *Journal of Bone and Joint Surgery*, May, 1952.

CHAMBERLAIN, W. E. *Low Back Pain.* Reprinted from *Proceedings of the California Academy of Medicine*, 1937-38.

MEYERDING, H. W. "Low Back-ache and Sciatic Pain Associated with Spondylolisthesis and Protruded Intervertebral Disk," *Journal of Bone and Joint Surgery*, 2:461, 1941.

KING, A. B. "Back Pain Due to Loose Facets of the Lower Lumbar Vertebrae," *Bulletin of the Johns Hopkins Hospital*, 97:3 (Sept., 1955), pp. 271-83.

HACKETT, G. S. *Joint Ligament Relaxation Treated by Fibro-Osseous Proliferation.* Springfield, Ill.: Thomas, 1956.

SHUMAN, DAVID. *Low Back Pain.* Philadelphia: Published by the author, 1958.

III. CURARE

New and Nonofficial Remedies, American Medical Association, 1950.

United States Pharmacopeia, 1950.

BENNETT, A. E. "Clinical Investigations with Curare in Organic Neurologic Disorders," *American Journal of Medical Science*, Vol. 202, 1941.

GILL, R. C. *White Water and Black Magic.* New York: Henry Holt and Co., 1940.

FULLER, JOHN D. "Use of Slowly Absorbed Suspension of d-Tubocurarine Chloride in Traumatic Injury," *Journal of the American Medical Association,* July 1, 1950.

JONEZ, H. D. "Multiple Sclerosis Treatment with Histamine and d-Tubocurarine," *Annals of Allergy,* vol. 6, 1948.

SHUMAN, D. "Physiology," *Osteopathic Profession,* Feb., 1951.

BLUMBERG, H., and GORDON, S. M.,"Comparison of Aqueous and Repository Tubocurarine for Muscle Relaxant Effectiveness and Toxicity in Rabbits," *Federation Proceedings,* 14, 1955, p. 319.

LIPOW, E. G. "Slowly Absorbed Tubocurarine Chloride in Orthopedics," *A.M.A. Archives of Surgery,* 66:312, 1953.

HAKLUYT, RICHARD. *The Principal Navigations, Voyages, Traffiques and Discoveries of The English Nation made by Sea or Over-land to the Remote and Farthest Distant Quarters of the Earth at any Time within the Compasse of these 1600 yeeres* (vol. X). New York: The Macmillan Co., 1904.

MALIA, E. R., *et al.* "Clinical Evaluation of Tubadil," *Journal of the American Medical Association,* 156:7, 1954.

HOBACK, W. "Repository Tubocurarine in Trauma," *Journal of the Tennessee State Medical Association,* 45:1 (1952), pp. 16-18.

THIEMEYER, J. S., and REED, E. F. "The Use of Tubadil (Repository Injection of Tubocurarine) in Acute Back Strain," *Clinical Orthopedics* #3. Philadelphia: J. B. Lippincott, 1954.

McINTYRE, A. R. *Curare, Its History, Nature and Clinical Use.* Chicago: Univ. of Chicago Press, 1947.

GRIFFITH, H. R. "The Use of Curare In Anesthesia And For Other Clinical Purposes," *Canadian Medical Association Journal,* 50:144, 1944.

KING, H. J. "Curare Alkaloids," *Journal of the Chemical Society* (London), 1935, p. 1381.

GILL, R. C. Personal communications to the authors.

GORDON, S. M. Personal communications to the authors.

215

IV. PSYCHOSOMATIC

LINN, L. "Psychosomatic Aspects of Backache," *Connecticut Medical Journal*, 20:4 (April, 1956), pp. 288-90.

ASHER, R. "Backache as a Psychosomatic Manifestation," *Practitioner* (London), 179 (Aug., 1957), p. 1070.

SULLIVAN, J. D. "Psychiatric Factors in Low Back Pain," *New York State Journal of Medicine* 55:2 (15 Jan., 1955), pp. 227-32.

BROWN, T., *et al.* "Psychological Factors in Low Back Pain," *New England Journal of Medicine*, 251:4 (22 July, 1954), pp. 123-8.

HOLMES, T. H. and WOLFF, H. G. "Life Situations, Emotions and Backache," *Psychosomatic Medicine*, 14:K8-33 (Jan.-Feb., 1952).

PAUL, T. "Psychosomatic Aspects of Low Back Pain," *Psychosomatic Medicine*, 12:116-124 (March-April, 1950).

WEISS, EDWARD, and ENGLISH, O. SPURGEON. *Psychosomatic Medicine*. Philadelphia: Saunders, 1957.

CANNON, WALTER B. *Bodily Changes in Pain, Hunger, Fear and Rage*. Boston: Charles T. Branford Co., 1953.

V. PROCAINE

CARNETT, J. B., and BATES, W. "Railway Spine," *Surgical Clinics in North America*, Dec., 1932.

JUDOVICH, B. D., and BATES, W. "Low Back Pain," *Industrial Medicine*, April, 1939.

———. *Segmental Neuralgia in Painful Syndromes* (2nd ed.). Philadelphia: F. A. Davis Co., 1946.

SHUMAN, D. "Low Back Pain," *Osteopathic Profession*, Nov., 1946.

DUTTON, W. F., and LAKE, G. B. *Parenteral Therapy*, Springfield, Ill.: Charles C. Thomas, 1936.

VI. LIFTS

BAILEY, H. W., and BECKWITH, C. G. "Short Leg and Spinal Anomalies," *Journal of the American Osteopathic Association,* March, 1937.

SCHWAB, W. A. "Principles of Manipulative Treatment," *Journal of the American Osteopathic Association,* Feb. & March, 1932.

BEAL, M. C. "A Review of the Short Leg Problem," *Journal of the American Osteopathic Association,* Oct., 1950.

PEARSON, W. M., *et al.* "A Progressive Study of School Children," *Journal of the American Osteopathic Association,* Nov., 1951.

VII. ON THE FUTILITY OF TRACTION FOR LOW BACK TREATMENT

ROTHENBERG, S. R., and associates. "Effect of Leg Traction on Ruptured Intervertebral Disk," *Surgery, Gynecology and Obstetrics,* May, 1953.

INDEX